# BEYOND THE SCREEN

## Youth Ministry for the Connected But Alone Generation

*Far and away one of the best youth
ministry books of the last twenty years.
~Kenda Creasy Dean*

## ANDREW ZIRSCHKY

**BEYOND THE SCREEN:**
**YOUTH MINISTRY FOR THE CONNECTED BUT ALONE GENERATION**

**Library of Congress Cataloging-in-Publication Data**

CIP Data has been requested.

15 16 17 18 19 20 21 22 23 24—10 9 8 7 6 5 4 3 2 1

MANUFACTURED IN THE UNITED STATES OF AMERICA

# CONTENTS

*For Evan and Anna*

*May you experience the presence of Christ and the communion
of the saints described in these pages.*

# ACKNOWLEDGMENTS

Thank you to my mentors at Princeton Seminary including Gordon Mikoski and Richard Osmer who were instrumental in inspiring the thinking and theology poured out in these pages. There are not enough words to express the debt that I owe Kenda Dean who has been a trusted advisor, mentor, and friend. She has believed in me (and this book) all the way along.

Tim Baker has been indispensable in providing direction to turn a rambling and protracted dissertation into an accessible and meaningful youth ministry resource. Thanks are also in order to Jack Radcliffe at Youth Ministry Partners and Abingdon Press for believing in this project and running the publishing gauntlet to make it happen.

My colleagues at the Center for Youth Ministry Training have been infinitely encouraging amidst my endless "writing retreat" absences: Thank you Deech, Lesleigh, Julia, Keeley, Margaret, and Kris. As well, my students from CYMT and Memphis Seminary should be recognized for their thoughtful feedback through various iterations of this book.

I owe my family, including my parents, spouse, and children, a tremendous debt for their patience and help through this process: Thank you Dwight, Linde, Kristina, Evan, and Anna.

I also need to thank my many friends who have journeyed with me at various points in this process, among them the Timothy Scholars from Princeton Seminary: Thank you Mindi, Erik, Adam, Andy, Mike, Jason, Drew, Nate, Christy, Blair, Stephen, Amanda, and Katie.

# INTRODUCTION

Teenagers do not want your technology. That simple claim challenges conventional youth ministry wisdom. Despite the popular conception that youth are ravenous consumers of all things digital, the reality is that youth are not nearly as enthralled by technology as we might believe. This may seem like a naïve claim considering the sheer number of hours that teenagers spend using cell phones, tablets, computers, and digital devices of all kinds. After all, the average teenager has 3.5 personal digital gadgets and spends 10.5 hours per day in mediated "screen time."[1] This would seem to indicate a passionate love for all things technological. However, teenage use of technology does not ultimately point to adolescent gadget hunger, but instead to a ravenous appetite for relationships—the deep, heartaching, knowing relationships that increasingly seem difficult to find in a fast-paced society separated by distance, speed, and sheer busyness. Teenagers, in their characteristic ability to turn culture on its head, have appropriated the very computer technologies sometimes blamed for communal breakdown, in an attempt to maintain constant presence and to commune with one another digitally. Teenagers have turned technology social and use social media to communicate seamlessly, endlessly—and maybe most surprising—meaningfully.

One of the central claims of this book is that the rise and dominance of social technology is a signpost that should help us see that teenagers are hungry for continuous, meaningful relationships with other humans and a kind of community not easily discovered in the disconnected landscape of modern American existence—alas, not easily discovered in our churches either.

## THE IRRELEVANCE OF RELEVANCE

This means that, in fact, many in the field of youth ministry have misread the significance of emerging Internet and mobile technologies, thinking that the church establishes relevance to the lives of teenagers simply through the act of adopting technology for use in ministry. In reality, teenagers are not looking for technology, app-savvy youth ministries, or mere connections. What is truly relevant to the lives of teenagers are relationships of depth and a community of people who "live present" to one another. Such a community of presence is precisely what the church is called by God to be and to offer to humanity; the scriptural word for such a community is *koinonia*, which can be translated as fellowship, sharing, or most poignantly—communion. The irony is that youth ministers who try to stay "relevant" by adopting the latest social media apps secure their own irrelevance if they fail to understand the true attraction of youth to social media and fail to offer the deep community that God intended and that youth long for. We need a path beyond the irrelevance of relevance, and we establish that by changing our focus from technology to ecclesiology.

## A QUESTION OF ECCLESIOLOGY

When we talk about social media in youth ministry, we often focus on strategies for using social apps to stay relevant. Some youth ministers laud the connective possibilities of social and mobile media, while others lament its impact on relationships, attention span, and adolescent faith. Currently, what almost all our discussions share is a focus on the technology: Is it good? Is it bad? How can we use it? Should we avoid it? These questions aren't wrong, but they make it easy to give all our attention to the nature of the technology, without giving proper focus to the nature of the church in a technological society.

This is the question worth examining: What does it mean for the church to live together as *koinonia* (communion) in the face of networked society? In other words, instead of merely examining social media from a Christian perspective, we must examine what it means to be the church in the social media age. By doing this we may be able to reclaim the church's God-ordained role of offering young people the intimacy that social apps promise but cannot deliver. Teenagers want neither technology nor mere connections with other people; however, they *are* longing for the intimate form of community and relational presence that, I will argue, is most characterized by the Christian understanding of *koinonia*—communion.

Therefore, this isn't yet another book about social media; this is ultimately a book about communion: what it is, how we have failed to offer it, and how it can transform the relationship of teenagers to the church in a digitally networked world. Set within the tradition of practical theology, our exploration will require understanding the way that teenagers use social media, along with the pressures that they (and truly, all of us) face in networked culture. This will be paired with theological exposition of Christian relationality so that our recommendations for youth ministry arise from the dynamic interplay of contextual reality and theological reflection.

Rather than focusing on tips for using social media, I want us to understand how our ministries can be better configured to reflect their God-given purpose and thereby more effectively minister to youth in a digital age. There is nothing wrong with, as Elizabeth Drescher put it, "engaging the potential of new digital social media for positive transformation in the church."[2] But I would argue the most powerful transformation for youth ministry is rooted, not in the potentials of new media, but in the potentials of living faithfully as *koinonia* in a networked world.

Many in youth ministry have paid attention to the technologies teenagers use to connect without pausing to understand why they connect the way they do. Consequently, the first three chapters give us new eyes for understanding what teens are seeking through their use of social media. In Chapter 1, we will examine how teenagers' use of social media attests to a desire for relationships of presence. In Chapter 2, we'll examine how social media permits teenagers to take their friends with them wherever they go in efforts to maintain relational contact. Chapter 3 explores how teenagers turn pithy status updates and trivial text messages into a language of intimacy on their quest for experiencing relationships of presence. In each chapter, suggestions are made for revising our youth ministry practice in light of cultural realities and theological considerations.

Chapters 4 and 5 introduce the social system of networked individualism that stands behind teenage use of social media. Every culture operates from a commonly held view of relational norms and social aspirations that some have called a "social operating system."[3] Networked individualism is the emerging social operating system of the digital age. Along with this operating system come demands that are placed upon its inhabitants. Chapter 4 inspects the basic features of networked individualism and compares it to previous social systems. Chapter 5 explores the demands placed upon teenagers if they hope to be socially successful in a networked world, and it sets forth some of the detrimental effects teenagers are likely to experience.

Beginning with Chapter 6, the book makes a turn and the reader will notice a pronounced movement toward biblical and theological engagement as we uncover the meaning of Christian *koinonia* for a networked age. In Chapter 6, we'll examine Paul's theology of *koinonia* through a close reading of 1 Corinthians 10–12. This lays the groundwork for Chapters 7–10, which explore Christian *koinonia* in contrast to the ailments of networked individualism. In conversation with the theological work of Jürgen Moltmann, each of these chapters engages one of the effects of networked individualism on youth and the ways in which *koinonia* directly contrasts and heals the experiences of teenagers in networked society. Chapter 7 explores faceless relationality in contrast to the depth of communion. Chapter 8 explores the anxiety teenagers experience in networked society in contrast to the unachieved belonging of *koinonia*. Chapter 9 contrasts the homogenous friendships of networked individualism with the diverse unity that God intends for Christian fellowship. The way in which networked individualism promotes selective sociality in contrast to the open embrace of Christian *koinonia* is the subject of Chapter 10. In each of these chapters, we'll examine practices that can lead us toward experiencing communion in the Holy Spirit.

Finally, in Chapter 11, we will look at the ways in which social media can become a location for the holy practices explored in earlier chapters. Such a view challenges exclusion-or-embrace perspectives on social media, and offers the possibility that the church can employ social media in ways that reflect its own operating system of communion in contrast to networked individualism. As such, social media can be transformed.

In an age in which the very structure and logic of human sociality is in flux, the importance of congregations and youth ministries "devoting themselves to the communion" (Acts 2:42) is of unparalleled importance.

Communion, understood in the depth and richness of the theological and scriptural tradition does not just stand in contrast to the networked sociality of our age, but also serves as a "hermeneutic of the gospel."[4] That's missiologist and theologian Lesslie Newbigin's phrase to describe how the life of the church can serve as a lens through which the message of Christ either makes sense (or does not) to the watching world.

If you peruse newsfeeds on teenagers and social media, you will find them filled with reports about bullying, loss of empathy, defamation, media-induced anxiety, the rise in teenage narcissism, Facebook-induced depression, and the increasing number of teenagers who feel alone. Headlines make it clear there is a deep need for something other than networked relationality. When the church lives as communion, we provide in our relationships together a distinct contrast to the dominant form of sociality in our time as we model radical love for one another and the world. Inviting youth into such a community can become a powerful form of youth ministry in networked culture. Forming teenagers' understanding and practice of social relationships is one of the most significant challenges for Christian formation in the contemporary world. Christian formation in the age of networks cannot be merely a matter of forming knowledge and personal piety. Discipleship must extend to forming youth into members of the body of Christ and inviting them to experience communion beyond connection—fellowship beyond the screen.

1. "Social Media and Mobile Internet Use Among Teens and Young Adults" (Pew Research Center, February 2010) at *http://www.pewinternet.org/files/old-media/Files/Reports/2010/PIP_Social_Media_and_Young_Adults_Report_Final_with_toplines.pdf*. In 2010 the Pew Internet and American Life Project found that teenagers on average own 3.5 devices from a list that included cell phones, Mp3 players, computers, and gaming devices. Also, "Generation M2: Media in the Lives of 8- to 18-Year-Olds," (Kaiser Family Foundation, January 2010) at *http://kff.org/other/event/generation-m2-media-in-the-lives-of/*. Teenagers spend nearly 10.5 hours of screen time daily.
2. *Tweet If You Heart Jesus: Practicing Church in the Digital Reformation,* by Elizabeth Drescher (Morehouse Publishing, 2011); xv.
3. *Networked: The New Social Operating System,* by Barry Wellman and Lee Rainie (MIT Press, 2014).
4. *The Gospel in a Pluralist Society,* by Lesslie Newbigin (Eerdmans Publishing, 1989); page 224.

*Note*: At the time of publication, all websites provided throughout this book were correct and operational.

Discipleship must extend to forming youth into members of the body of Christ and inviting them to experience communion beyond connection—fellowship beyond the screen.

# BATTERIES NOT DESIRED:

## SOCIAL MEDIA AND THE TEENAGE SEARCH FOR PRESENCE

"What we need is more video," the youth pastor declared as we brainstormed about the problem of youth inattention at Wednesday night gatherings. The room of adult leaders quieted some to listen to him. "Instead of standing up there talking, let's video ourselves—the students will pay better attention to the screen than to a real person. Video always attracts their attention," he stated passionately. The youth pastor was particularly proud of his newfound insight, but I shifted uncomfortably in my seat. He had just made appeal to what I call the Moth Myth—the assumption that teenagers, like moths, are attracted to things that plug-in and light up.

The Moth Myth is a reasonable assumption considering the average American teenager owns 3.5 digital gadgets and daily engages in screen time equivalent to roughly two months of youth group attendance.[1]

No wonder many youth workers believe that the latest technological innovations and social media hold the key to more effective ministry with young people. So, we outfit our youth rooms with the latest digital gadgets and turn to apps such as Instagram and Twitter as "ministry essentials," while hoping to attract teens with relevant ministry.

As I sat in the weekly youth leader meeting at our large New Jersey church, there was good reason to believe the Moth Myth was true. The meeting had been convened as part of our ongoing battle for youth to silence their cell phones and listen. It seemed that tearing teenagers away from their devices to pay attention to a speaker at the front of the room was impossible, regardless of our use of humor, stories, and gimmicks. Despite my protest, the consensus in the room was that we should fight fire with fire: Grab teenagers' attention away from the glow of their smartphones with a bigger and brighter screen. It was decided that next week's sermon would be prerecorded. "It works for Rob Bell in those Nooma videos!" the youth pastor added as the meeting dispersed, "It's gonna work for us, too!"

The following week was my turn to speak at Wednesday night youth group. A few days prior, armed with a ragtag film crew, we set out to record the sermon. I gave my opening illustration while leaning against a tree, before the wannabe film director (the middle school pastor) called "Cut!" He then moved me to a crouched position on some outdoor stairs, sunlight streaming in radiant bands behind me. I made it through my first point before I was "Cut!" again. The starts and stops continued for an hour before I was dismissed so that the film team could edit the clips into something usable—presumably something that made me look and sound more like Rob Bell.

That Wednesday evening at youth group, with lights low, my sermon played out on the big screen—despite the fact I was physically standing in the back of the room and ready to deliver it in person. The assumption was that technology will hold teenagers' attention better than someone upfront talking, and the impulse was correct—to a point. Youth did stare at the screen and their chatter did quiet. It was not unlike the effect of being in a stadium and choosing to watch the projected image rather than the live action itself.[2] Yet, this effect waned quickly and, by the end of the night, students returned to their devices. In fact, within a few weeks, the level of conversation in the group actually increased because there was no one upfront whom they might offend, only a projected video image.

It was surreal watching myself preach a prerecorded message, so I quietly slipped outside. As I stood there in the air of a cool spring evening, watching a moth flit and flick against the sodium-green glow of a security light, I realized the fatal flaw in our thinking. We had failed to realize that teenagers' attraction to smartphones, laptops, games, and gadgets is not a function of the glowing screen, but a function of what or who is on the other end. Moths flit against light bulbs out of pure phototactic (light-loving) attraction, but teenagers are searching for something else— something beyond the screen.[3]

In early twenty-first-century America, the glow of the screen gives young people access to a world of connective relationships not easily replicated in our disconnected face-to-face society. Teenagers are not moths, but in viewing them as such, we have paid attention to the technology around which they gather and ignored the distinction between how they connect and why they connect. We know they use Instagram and Snapchat, Twitter and text messaging, but we have done a poor job of understanding the deeper reasons why teenagers use social media. And it appears those reasons may have little to do with bright lights and shiny objects.

## THE DRAW TO SOCIAL MEDIA

Increasingly empirical research suggests that teenage use of technology points beyond an adolescent hunger for gadgets toward a hunger for relationships of presence. After three years of research funded by the MacArthur Foundation, digital ethnographer danah boyd (yes, her name is all lowercase) and her fellow researchers concluded that teenagers use social media to establish "full-time intimate communities" that provide for always-on communication and relationships.[4] Such communities differ significantly from the communities that teenagers experience daily in highly mobile (and consequently disconnected) face-to-face society. Those communities are fleeting and transitory. This is true in the sense that our communities change from month to month and year to year, but it's also more immediately true that the access to any given community changes at numerous points throughout the day. The community of middle school homeroom convenes for fifty minutes. A teenager has access to her community of best friends for thirty minutes during lunch. The community of the sports team gathers for a few hours each afternoon during the school week, but only in season. The cabin of tight-knit summer campers convenes once a year. The community of youth group meets for an hour, once or twice a week. Even the community of the family convenes only a few hours a day in most American households. Teenagers experience a multitude of fleeting and transitory communities and relationships daily, but social media allows them to enact relationships and draw upon the support of communities that are effervescent, always-on, and full-time.

These communities can feel intimate in contrast to the loose anonymity of the occasional communities convened at school, church, or elsewhere. Facebook is filled with one's friends. Instagram is populated by those you follow and the people who follow you. When a teenager launches a social media app, the people they encounter are known friends with whom they have history. Showing up to youth group, on the other hand? Who knows whom they might encounter, or if anyone will greet and remember them.

Another social media researcher, Craig Watkins, finds that youth appropriate technology, not primarily for its entertainment value or cool factor, but because of its potential to foster "presence-in-absence"— the ability to be with friends despite physical separation.[5] Through hundreds of interviews with teenagers and college students, Watkins discovered that their commitment to technology is "driven primarily by their commitment to each other and a desire to stay connected."[6] The technology itself garnered little interest from teenagers.

There is of course some significance in the fact that Instagram and text messaging are the communication choices for teenagers, but Watkins says the greater significance is the "expression of intimacy" and the experience of presence in absence that such media offer. Presence in absence is an important experience because teenagers so often encounter absence in presence. The feeling of being alone in a crowd is the feeling of absence in presence. It's an increasingly common experience at school, church, and even home as the pace of life increases, as we navigate large, impersonal institutions, and as we depend more and more on technology to mediate our interactions with one another. (There's an irony, of course, that teenagers are turning to technology to experience presence when technology has contributed to the impersonal and faceless interactions they experience.) Yes, we still trade social pleasantries with the clerk in the grocery checkout line, but there isn't a relationship there. She interacts with us, and we interact with her, but in a faceless fashion—as if it doesn't matter if any of us have a face, a name, or a story.[7] And we experience absence in the midst of presence.

Digital ethnographers seem to agree that the dominant practices of social media usage by teenagers are friendship-driven not tech-driven.[8] Take away the connectivity of their devices, turn off text messaging and remove their contact list, and teenagers are far less interested in smartphones. In other words, batteries are not required, but meaningful and continuous social contact is required by young people with an unquenchable desire to be present with others. boyd summarizes it best: "Most teens aren't addicted to social media; if anything, they're addicted to each other."[9] And if we are going to call it "addiction," suggests boyd, we need to simultaneously recognize that it arises from a healthy desire to connect to others; it is "part of the human condition."[10] In a world of transitory and fleeting experiences of relationality, maybe we should be happy that teenagers are seeking to hold onto some kind of relational permanence.

In light of what digital ethnographers are discovering, it should be clear that our gratuitous use of technology does little to meet the needs of youth. Many within the church misread teens' burgeoning use of social technologies as a love for all things digital, and so the church tries to woo them with connections to slick websites, Facebook pages, Twitter accounts, and the latest technology. Or we install larger-than-life video screens and broadcast prerecorded messages like my church in New Jersey. The notion that youth, like moths, are attracted to things that plug-in and light up is truly a myth. None of these approaches are relevant to the heart cry of contemporary teenagers.

Neither does our gratuitous use of technology testify to the church as the transformed body of Christ marked by the depth of our communion together. Teenagers' profound quest to experience presence in networked culture is best addressed by the church through attending to our God-given charge to live in communion together. Teenagers are not content to be wooed with technology, nor are they content to simply be in physical proximity to others. Contemporary teenagers are seeking something more than mere connection. They're seeking presence—an experience of sharing in which they are alongside, available, with, within, and known to one another. The Christian term for such an experience is the Greek word *koinonia*, often reduced to fellowship, but most appropriately translated in English as communion. In understanding the nature of communion and the practices that prepare the congregation as fertile ground for the transforming work of the Holy Spirit so that we may be communion, the church offers young people an alternative to the mere connections of networked culture—and helps them find the experience of presence they seek.

Christian community is supposed to be rooted in *koinonia*, an intimate intertwining and sharing of life in which Christ is present with us as we are present with one another.[11] The body of Christ is a bold vision of "full-time intimate community," but a vision that has been too often neglected, especially when considering the nature of youth ministry.[12]

## SEEKING THE PRESENCE OF FRIENDS

Saying that teens use social media for meaningful relationships and to experience social presence runs counter to popular perceptions and dominant narratives. Popular sentiment is that teenagers use technology to avoid social contact by hiding behind their phones. But such notions are a misread of the actions and experiences of teens, and research shows that teenagers primarily use social media to maintain persistent social presence with those who are important to them. Getting this right is crucial or we risk responding to youth and social media in ways that miss the point.

While the technology exists to connect perfect strangers who are in the same vicinity, so far those technologies have not proven popular among teenagers.[13] Certainly a subset of young adults have been drawn to hookup apps such as Tinder, but especially with teenagers, researchers find that mobile technologies do not produce indiscriminate relationships but rather "reinforce existing social relations."[14] Consider, for example, that the average fourteen-year-old sends/receives approximately one hundred text messages a day—that's an enormous amount of communication.[15] (Imagine how long you'd have been in detention if you passed one hundred notes a day in school!) But if you imagine that those one hundred messages are flying to a myriad of friends and digital acquaintances near and far, then you're imagination is incorrect. Research reveals that teenagers are usually communicating with a relatively small number of people—as few as three to five close friends who are usually nearby.[16] The ongoing exchange of messages feeds a sense of social presence when teenagers are physically separated from their closest friends.

Teenagers do in fact meet new friends online through social media, but this activity is outmatched by their use of social media to stay in touch with existing friends. In 2007, Pew found that half of teens used social networking sites to make new friends, and eight years later the number had ticked up to 57 percent of teenagers who reported making at least one new friend online.[17] That's not insignificant, but compare that to 91 percent of teens who say their dominant use of social media is to stay in touch with existing friends.[18] Teenagers are not primarily trolling for new friends online, rather they're trying to maintain constant contact with the close friends they already have. Even when they do make new friends online, the vast majority of these new contacts are friends of friends, not the random strangers portrayed in media reports.[19] One middle school boy explained it this way: "I use iMessaging and like I joined a group with a couple of my friends and my friend invited one of his friends. And then we all just kind of met through the group chat."[20]

For the most part, teenagers use technology to maintain relationships and build full-time intimate community with friends they've met offline and online, even as they attempt to maintain a sense of presence with a few of their closest friends. They're interested in friendship.

This is one reason why teens' adoption rate for Twitter has been so slow. Twitter was one of the first widely used social media platforms that wasn't driven by early teenage adoption, and even today only a third of teenagers use Twitter compared to an astounding 71 percent who use Facebook—despite the reported abandonment of Facebook by teens.[21] What accounts for the lackluster adoption of Twitter by teenagers, even as they flock to other new social platforms, such as Instagram? Simply, Twitter is less suited for socializing and fostering relationships (especially with those whom one knows face-to-face) than it is for sharing information in a social fashion—and teens know this.

"While many adults find value in socializing with strangers," writes danah boyd, "teenagers are more focused on socializing with people they know personally and celebrities that they adore."[22] Indeed, where adults tend to become intrigued by the socially shared information that technology can provide, teens are more about the intimacy that technology can foster. Teenagers tend to use social media to continue the bonds of already existing offline relationships, and to foster deeper levels of friendship and intimacy as they pick up a few new online friends along the way. As Watkins and others report, teens' true interests are "the people and the relationships the technology provides access to"[23] and Twitter is less capable than other services in this regard.

## FRIENDS MORE THAN FADS

While adults often conceive of teens as early adopters seeking out the latest cool social app, the reality is that teens adopt technology based upon their desire to connect with friends. Remember, the killer app for teenagers remains text messaging, a twenty-five-year-old technology that lacks any of the bells and whistles of modern social apps. Nearly nine out of ten trade texts with friends.[24] What explains their interest? Availability and privacy. Their friends are available via text, and it's generally private. Sleek apps and novel features aren't necessary.

Facebook makes an interesting case study to show that teens are after friends more than fads. Longstanding predictions that Facebook would be deemed uncool by teens were finally fulfilled in 2013 when Pew reported that teen distaste for Facebook was growing. At the same time, Piper Jaffray found that only 23 percent of them described Facebook as the "most important social media site" for teenagers—a drop from 42 percent who said the same a year previous.[25] Yet, the Pew study didn't find that teenagers had grown bored with the technology, but rather they were fed up with the relational drama perpetuated by Facebook. Nevertheless, the Pew study revealed that teens largely continue to use the service (or at least maintain profiles) because it remains a viable way to connect to offline friends.[26] When Pew surveyed teens again two years later, Facebook had lost even more of its cool factor, yet remained the most widely adopted social platform among teens (71 percent are users) despite the social cachet of apps like Instagram and Snapchat. For teenagers, tech is about relationships before cool.

## STILL HANGING OUT

Not only do teenagers use social media to stay in touch with close friends and to foster a sense of presence with them, without much concern for the latest technology, but they also use the technology to arrange in-person gatherings. In other words, teens use social media to foster further social interactions and not to avoid them. Facebook and text message are enormously popular ways for youth to coordinate and congregate—not just in digital space, but physical space as well. In fact, 72 percent of young people use social networking sites to "make plans with friends."[27]

The displacement hypothesis (the theory that "time spent with media takes people away from human interaction and breaks down social connectedness and community") does not describe well the reality of adolescent interactions in networked culture.[28] In-person encounters are holding steady (despite the increasing difficulty of teenagers to gather physically because of societal restrictions) while text messaging and other forms of digital contact increase.[29]

Additionally, while some fear the rise of disembodied community carried on through digital means, teenagers (the ones branded "digital natives") by far and away reject the notion of completely online community. A study of adolescent girls with social networking profiles found the vast majority said they still prefer in-person communication to communicating with friends via social networking technologies.[30] The majority of teenagers and young adults (84 percent) disagree that online relationships can be just as fulfilling as offline relationships.[31]

Despite fears that young people would be quick to abandon face-to-face relationships, the data indicate quite the opposite: Teenagers are not attempting social displacement but are using online contact to augment and strengthen their offline relationships, all while gaining some online friends along the way.

Youth ministry, and the church as a whole, should take notice that teens are not seeking the latest technology, nor are they seeking to avoid communities of presence. But, in fact, they're searching for a community of persistent presence that is more robust and dependable than many of the transitory communities they encounter in-person on a daily basis.

## RECLAIMING COMMUNION IN YOUTH MINISTRY

At my church in New Jersey, we thought students wanted smoke, lights, and a brilliant screen. We kept giving them more compelling technology and couldn't understand why they still were distracted. They wanted to be engrossed in relationships of present presence, but we couldn't see that.

When we replaced the Wednesday evening speaker with a recorded video message, our ministry had not risen to the heights of relevance, but plummeted to the depths of irrelevance: The youth staff prided themselves on producing quality video, but teenagers were longing for presence. The youth staff boasted about the amazing lights installed for the worship band, but teenagers were seeking always-on relationships. We spent hours crafting relevant teaching points and dramatic object lessons, all while teenagers were seeking full-time intimate community. We convinced them to remain hushed and facing forward, while they sought to be known by others. We provided little of what they hungered for and even less of what the body of Christ is called to be.

Youth ministry finds its roots in Christian education, a field that in many corners has been more concerned with instilling biblical knowledge and Christian morals than a holistic experience of Christian formation. Those things matter, but the church as a gathered community is first and foremost a people in whom the life of Christ and the bond of Christ is supposed to be lived out. The early church was defined by *koinonia*—its operating system, its way of life together—far more than it was defined as a gathering of learners. To be formed in Christ was to be formed within the body of Christ. In a world of social media, it's time that we reclaim the peculiar relationality of the church and move youth ministry beyond a ministry of informing, or beyond a ministry of wholesome Christian activity, toward a ministry of presence—a ministry in which teens experience communion.

But let's be honest: This will not be an easy shift. Most youth ministers have given little thought to inviting youth into the *koinonia* of the church. More problematic, in many congregations there isn't much *koinonia* to invite youth into anyway! Ultimately, then, the task of youth ministry becomes about reigniting a concern for genuine Christian community throughout the congregation—in both the youth ministry properly speaking, as well as beyond.

That is certainly a large task, but it's not impossible, because ultimately experiencing communion together is not a human task at all. The transformation of a congregation—or youth ministry—from a mere collection of people into communion is the work of the Holy Spirit. Our role is to pray and prepare for such transformation through enacting communal practices that—like the sails of a ship—can be filled by the Spirit. When sailors hoist the mainsail, it's a practice that signals they're ready for their bobbing hunk of wood to be transformed into the sailing vessel it was created to be. The practice of raising the sail doesn't transform the movement of the ship—the wind does that—but without readying the sail, the wind will blow right by. If we hope to experience communion together as the church, there are practices that function similarly to hoisting the sails, readying us for the work of the Spirit. In the pages ahead, I refer to these as epicletic practices. An epiclesis is a prayer that calls down the Holy Spirit ("Come, Holy Spirit, Come"), and an epicletic practice is any human activity that functions as a prayer by pointing toward and participating in the very transformation we hope the Holy Spirit to enact in us. We will learn more about these practices that I call "epicletic" (not to be confused with epileptic!); but for now it's enough to recognize that these are practices that prepare congregations to be transformed by the Holy Spirit.

# REJECTING THE MOTH MYTH

It's time that we reject the Moth Myth and stop our gratuitous use of technology in hopes of attracting teenagers. While there's nothing inherently wrong with using a variety of technologies in youth ministry, the amount of time, money, and energy spent trying to stay abreast of technological change tends to suck resources that could be better spent or used in other ways. More to the point, gratuitous use of technology isn't necessarily destructive, but it's likely to deceive us into thinking that we're busying ourselves with relevant forms of ministry. The screens on the wall and the well-liked Instagram account might very well give you a false sense of security that you're doing ministry that matters to the deepest longings of teenagers. Don't believe it.

Consider whether you have been employing technology to attract teens rather than to connect them more deeply and profoundly with one another and to the larger body of Christ. If you stripped away the technology from your ministry, would teens be any less known to one another? If the answer is no, then chances are that you've been adding technology to wow rather than to deeply connect teenagers with one another.

Do the technologies you employ assist youth and adults to enter relationships of knowing and presence with one another? Have you actually seen relationships blossom through the technologies on which you spend time and money?

There's no foolproof test for being beholden to the Moth Myth, but honestly answering such questions will help in reflecting upon your personal tendencies. Rejecting the Moth Myth by no means requires jettisoning technology. It does require that we give more attention and effort to fostering relationships of presence in our ministries than we do to the technological flourishes that satisfy our need for appearing cool or relevant.

Taking time to prayerfully reflect before blindly adopting technology can become an epicletic practice through which our ministries are shaped even as the reflection itself becomes an enacted prayer for the Holy Spirit's transforming power. Rejecting the use of technology that doesn't enhance the ability of youth and adults to know and care for one another can actually become an epicletic practice through which you prayerfully express your desire to be a community of presence with one another.

## DISRUPTING FACE-FORWARD MINISTRY

Teen social media usage reveals a population longing for presence, but we've largely interpreted it as a longing for apps and gadgets. As such, many congregations have made adjustments to youth ministry gatherings and all-church worship services by incorporating technology. However, the better adjustment would be incorporating relational interaction.

We are accustomed to thinking that in-person gatherings are inherently more meaningful than socializing through digital means, but that is not the case if our face-to-face interactions fail the test of presence. Just because we have convened together doesn't mean that teenagers will experience belonging, intimacy, and presence. Face-forward ministry is a matter of worshiping, learning, or even playing together at arm's-length: being in proximity to one another, but not experiencing presence together. There is a particular face-forward orientation in modern Christian worship that spills over into almost every other Christian gathering, from potlucks to youth group to Sunday school. We might sing the same songs and pray the same prayers, but we remain facing forward and anonymous to one another. Anonymity may be fine for the theater or the sporting arena, but when it pervades the church, we ultimately slip away from being a community of brothers and sisters in Christ.

The answer is not moving our interactions online, but instead recapturing the depth and meaning of gathering together as the body of Christ. And, for many churches, this may need to extend to the sanctuary but likely needs to begin in the youth room.

You may be saying: "Wait a second! Our youth ministry is not a face-forward ministry! We include all kinds of interaction at youth group, and we practice active learning in Sunday school. And we have small groups!" Not so fast.

Most youth ministries include a lot of interactivity, but very little true relational interaction among teens. I used to run a highly interactive

Sunday morning program at a church in southern Idaho. The opening was filled with games, contests, and laughter. The morning lesson encouraged the crowd of students to respond to the material being presented. But truth be told, what we did was modeled after *The Tonight Show*. It was highly interactive, but still it was possible for teens to walk away having responded to the person leading the group but without interacting relationally with anyone else.

Similarly, many Sunday school classes include active learning in which the teenagers move, talk, and roleplay. But often they are interacting with objects and ideas, and only on a cursory basis with one another. While it's not uncommon to begin or end class with a personal sharing time, often the focus quickly shifts to learning the "material" rather than being present with one another.

Small groups are supposed to be the ultimate fix to the face-forward mentality. Rather than the guru up front, they feature the guide on the side. Each member is supposed to be present and active in the experience, sharing self with the group. But in reality, small groups often maintain the face-forward mentality in which a group leader encourages relational interaction only to the degree that it advances the Bible study agenda for the day.

Despite our best efforts, we slide toward face-forward gatherings in which there is only cursory relational interaction because, despite the longing of teenagers to experience the presence of others, it "feels weird" to do anything more than face forward with the people at church. We should point out that gathering to worship and celebrate as the body of Christ and *not* interacting is actually what should feel weird!

The same kinds of practices that might dislodge youth ministries from a face-forward mentality can work throughout the entire congregation. Extending a greeting time or passing of the peace into a guided time of discussion and encouragement is one way to shake youth and adults loose from the face-forward mentality. Inviting youth into an extended time of guided sharing and prayer with a small group can shake our face-forward mentality. Interacting as groups and classes outside of scheduled times can foster relational presence in class sessions.

One of the most powerful experiences of dislodging the face-forward mentality occurred in our youth group where, for a month, we celebrated the Lord's Supper together weekly. We patterned our celebration after the tradition of a San Diego church visited by one of our students. In that church, worshippers are invited each week to receive the Lord's Supper and then to turn and serve the person next to them. "The body of Christ broken for you," declares the teenager to senior adult. "The blood of Christ shed for you," intones the homeless man to the church board member. This seems like an incredibly minor modification to the regular celebration, but it had profound effects as students were forced to face one another as members of Christ rather than facing forward.

Even though the suggestions above are truly minor adjustments, they're likely to create significant disruption and discomfort. That's a good thing. At the same time that these disruptive practices move us away from our forward-facing stance, they also operate as epicletic practices. For a youth ministry (or congregation) willing to attempt practices such as these, they function as prayers asking for the Holy Spirit to transform their very community by pointing toward and participating in the kind of *koinonia* they hope to become together.

1. "Social Media & Mobile Internet Use Among Teens and Young Adults" at *http://www.pewinternet. org/files/old-media/Files/Reports/2010/PIP_Social_Media_and_Young_Adults_Report_Final_with_ toplines.pdf*. Also, "Generation M2: Media in the Lives of 8- to 18-Year-Olds" at *http://kff.org/other/ event/generation-m2-media-in-the-lives-of/*.
2. "We Are the Jumbotron Generation," in *Yahoo Sports: The PostGame*, Feb. 1, 2011 at *http://www. thepostgame.com/homepage/201102/we-are-jumbotron-generation*.
3. There are numerous hypotheses about why moths are attracted to light. For a discussion, see *http:// science.howstuffworks.com/environmental/life/zoology/insects-arachnids/question675.htm*.
4. "Friendship," by danah boyd, in *Hanging Out, Messing Around, and Geeking Out: Kids Living and Learning with New Media*, by Mizuko Ito (MIT Press, 2010); page 84.
5. "Friendship," boyd, in *Hanging Out*, Ito, pages 79-116. Also, *The Young and the Digital*, by Craig Watkins (Beacon Press, 2010); pages 48-74.
6. *The Young and the Digital*, Watkins, page 74.
7. I am indebted to theologian David Ford for the concept of a faceless society explored in his excellent volume, *Self and Salvation: Being Transformed* (Cambridge University Press, 1999).
8. "Friendship" boyd, in *Hanging Out*, Ito, page 80.
9. *It's Complicated: The Social Lives of Networked Teens,* by danah boyd (Yale University Press, 2014); page 80.
10. *It's Complicated,* boyd, page 80.
11. See 1 Corinthians 10:16-18.
12. See 1 Corinthians 12:26.

13. "Teens, Social Media and Privacy" (Pew Research Center, May 2013) at *http://www.pewinternet. org/files/2013/05/PIP_TeensSocialMediaandPrivacy_PDF.pdf.* While 16 percent of teenage users allow social media posts to be tagged with their location, Pew researchers found that most teens are "for the most part quite wary of sharing their location," especially when it pertains to people they do not know having that information. Other teens in the study assumed that location services should be used with friends only and are thus somewhat redundant; as one participant said, "[I don't share my location] because it seems unnecessary. If someone wants to know where you are, they can ask."

14. *Personal, Portable, Pedestrian: Mobile Phones in Japanese Life,* by Mizuko Ito, Daisuke Okabe, and Misa Matsuda (MIT Press, 2006); page 9. Ito notes that heavy mobile media usage actually reinforces ties between close friends and families. Also, "Personal Relationships: On and Off the Internet," by Jeffrey Boase and Barry Wellman (Cambridge University Press, 2006) at *http://www.academia. edu/2983696/Personal_relationships_On_and_off_the_Internet.*

15. "Teens, Smartphones, and Texting," by Amanda Lenhard (Pew Research Center, March 2012) at *http://www.pewinternet.org/files/old-media//Files/Reports/2012/PIP_Teens_Smartphones_and_Texting. pdf.* In 2012, the median number of text messages sent/received by youth ages 14-17 was 100. The median sent by those 12-13 was 30. The median of all teen text messaging users was 60. When taking "average" to be the mean, the numbers jump to an average of 167 text messages sent/received daily. This is because some demographics send significantly more text messages than others; for example, the mean for girls ages 14-17 was 187 text messages a day!

16. *Personal, Portable, Pedestrian,* Ito, page 9. It has been confirmed in numerous countries that "youth send the majority of their mobile text messages to a group of three to five intimates."

17. "Social Networking Websites and Teens," by Amanda Lenhart and Mary Madden (Pew Research Center, January 2007) at *http://www.pewinternet.org/2007/01/07/social-networking-websites-and-teens/.* Also, "Teens, Technology and Friendships," by Lenhart, A., Smith, A., Anderson, M., Duggan, M., Perrin, A. (Pew Research Center, August 2015) at *http://www.pewinternet.org/2015/08/06/teens-technology-and-friendships/.*

18. "Teens, Social Media and Privacy" (Pew Research Center, May 2013) at *http://www.pewinternet. org/files/2013/05/PIP_TeensSocialMediaandPrivacy_PDF.pdf.*

19. "Teens, Social Media and Privacy" (Pew Research Center, May 2013) at *http://www.pewinternet. org/files/2013/05/PIP_TeensSocialMediaandPrivacy_PDF.pdf.*

20. "Social Networking Websites and Teens," by Amanda Lenhart and Mary Madden (Pew Research Center, January 2007) at *http://www.pewinternet.org/2007/01/07/social-networking-websites-and-teens/;* also *http://www.pewinternet.org/2015/08/06/chapter-1-meeting-hanging-out-and-staying-in-touch-the-role-of-digital-technology-in-teen-friendships/.*

21. "Teens, Technology and Friendships," by Lenhart, A., Smith, A., Anderson, M., Duggan, M., Perrin, A. (Pew Research Center, August 2015) at *http://www.pewinternet.org/2015/08/06/ teens-technology-and-friendships/;* also *http://www.pewinternet.org/2015/04/09/teens-social-media-technology-2015/.*

22. *Why Youth (Heart) Social Network Sites: The Role of Networked Publics in Teenage Social Life,* by danah boyd, at *http://www.danah.org/papers/WhyYouthHeart.pdf;* page 5.

23. *The Young and the Digital,* Watkins, page 74.

24. "Teens, Technology and Friendships," by Lenhart, A., Smith, A., Anderson, M., Duggan, M., Perrin, A. (Pew Research Center, August 2015) at *http://www.pewinternet.org/2015/08/06/teens-technology-and-friendships/.*

25. "Teens, Technology and Friendships," Smith, Anderson, Duggan, Perrin. Also, "Taking Stock with Teens," by Piper Jaffray at *http://www.piperjaffray.com/2col.aspx?id=287&releaseid=1863548.*

26. "Teens, Social Media and Privacy," (Pew Research Center, May 2013) at *http://www.pewinternet. org/files/2013/05/PIP_TeensSocialMediaandPrivacy_PDF.pdf.*

27. "Social Networking Websites and Teens," by Amanda Lenhart and Mary Madden (Pew Research Center, January 2007) at *http://www.pewinternet.org/2007/01/07/social-networking-websites-and-teens/*.

28. *The 21st Century Media (R)evolution: Emergent Communication Practices*, by Jim Macnamara (Peter Lang, 2010); page 84.

29. "Teens, Texting, and Social Isolation" (Pew Research Center, May 2010) at *http://www.pewinternet. org/2010/05/03/teens-texting-and-social-isolation/*. Pew found that face-to-face interactions held steady between 2006 and 2009 while text messaging use skyrocketed. Also, "The Networked Nature of Community: Online and Offline" by Barry Wellman, Jeffrey Boase, and Wenhong Chen in *It & Society 1*, No. 1 (2002); pages 151-165. Wellman et al. conclude that "rather than operating at the expense of the 'real' face-to-face world, [the Internet] is a part of it, with people using all means of communication to connect with friends and relatives. The Internet is another means of communication, which is being integrated into the regular patterns of social life." For a discussion on how inexperience going online can temporarily contribute to a decrease in face-to-face interaction, and a connection between personality type (introvert/extrovert) and similarity in social media usage, see "Personal Relationships: On and Off the Internet," by Jeffrey Boase and Barry Wellman, in *The Cambridge Handbook of Personal Relationships*, edited by Daniel Perlman and Anita L. Vangelisti (Cambridge University Press, 2006).

30. "Who's That Girl?" (Girl Scout Research Institute, 2010) at *http://www.girlscouts.org/research/pdf/ gsri_social_media_fact_sheet.pdf*.

31. *The Young and the Digital*, Watkins, page 60.

*Note*: At the time of publication, all websites provided throughout this book were correct and operational.

Where adults tend to become intrigued by the socially shared information that technology can provide, teens are more about the intimacy the technology can foster.

# "TAKING MY FRIENDS WITH ME":

## LIFE IN THE DIGITAL DIASPORA

"I don't buy it," one middle-aged father complained at a workshop I was leading for parents of teenagers. With arms folded to signal his discontent, he laid out his killer question: "If teens crave all this presence and relationship stuff you're talking about, then why are they using social media at all? Explain that."

It's a valid question, and one that comes up often: Why use social technology in a search for experiences of presence? Why not, you know, just be present, forgo the technology, and simply hang out like teenagers used to?

One simple answer is that technology allows teens to experience presence in absence when present presence isn't possible. And society is increasingly regulating and restricting the activities and movements of teenagers such that "present presence" is less possible than it used to be.

## ESCAPING SOLITARY CONFINEMENT THROUGH SOCIAL MEDIA

danah boyd notes that American teenagers spend the greater part of their existence in environments tightly controlled and structured by adults.[1] Most American high schools begin early in the morning (the bus picks up in my suburban Nashville neighborhood before 6:30 A.M.); and when school lets out in the late afternoon, teens are shuttled off to sports, clubs, or other extracurricular events. Considering that teenagers often live miles from their closest friends (whose schedules are also tightly programmed), it is easy to see how the weekday schedule can feel like solitary confinement for the relationally hungry adolescent. In much of America, teens are geographically bound by the lack of widespread access to easy public transportation systems and increasingly rigid driver's licensing laws that exclude teenagers from the ability of easy movement, notes boyd.[2] Add this to increasingly common curfew laws, and the decision of many suburban malls to ban teenagers without the accompaniment of a parent, and the end result is that youth have limited access to public spaces.

Consequently, teenagers must become creative in order to find ways to communicate and be together. Whenever subjected to systems and structures that prevent socializing, it is human nature to employ technology to subvert the system. I was reminded of this on a flight from Philadelphia to Memphis when I found myself seated next to an older gentleman named Leo, a Vietnam War veteran and an expert at using technology to "subvert the system."

Leo was not, however, an expert at using the latest gadgets. As I took my seat, he was visibly perplexed by his smartphone, pushing buttons and turning it around in his hand. "Do you have any idea how to unlock these things?" he finally inquired. "You're a young guy. Can you figure this out?"

Somehow it has become a societal assumption that if your gadget isn't working you should turn to the youngest person in the room—as if children are imbued with a magical gift for speaking to technological gadgets that fades ever so slowly with age. Without a teenager in clear view, my thirty-something self was going to have to suffice for this poor man's tech support.

While I fiddled with his phone, Leo told me war stories about receiving the Congressional Medal of Honor after spending six years as a POW in Vietnam. In captivity, Leo had been housed near other American POWs, but a concrete cell block prevented easy communication between them. With nothing but time on his hands, and living in what amounted to solitary confinement, Leo created a system of knocks and taps that became a makeshift communication system for the prisoners, allowing them to communicate without detection by their captors. The result was the ability to subvert the rigid structure under which they lived and maintain social contact. "That tap-tap-tap was often our only way to be together," Leo told me.

As I handed Leo's now-working phone back to him (I didn't fix it, but we did find a teenager in the back of the plane!), it dawned on me that Leo's system of taps has significant overlap with what teenagers are doing with mobile devices and social media: They are subverting the structured reality of their lives in order to communicate. Where Leo had used simple technology to escape the relational isolation of his captivity, in a similar fashion young people employ social technologies to escape the adult structured (and monitored) reality of their lives. They're using technology and their own tap-tap-tapping to alleviate loneliness as they search for presence with one another.

Text messaging and other forms of mobile communication operate as ways in which teenagers can subvert adult-structured environments in low-key or undetected ways. Yes, many teenagers can tap out a text message in class without detection, but the real promise of mobile social devices is enabling teenagers to hang out in groups without needing the confined space of a mall, school, or church.[3] Where previous technologies allowed friends to connect in private, the Internet allows teens to create virtual gathering places where multiple youth can congregate and communicate without adult monitoring even while they are physically present in adult-regulated spaces.[4] Far from being a mere diversion, social media is a lifeline through which teenagers are able to maintain and enhance a social presence together amidst the loneliness and social isolation of exurbia. Not only does social media allow youth to subvert the limitations placed upon them by society, but it also allows them to overcome the boundaries of geography in their pursuit of presence.

## "TAKING MY FRIENDS WITH ME"

Miranda was bored out of her mind with the discussion unfolding around her, but completely engrossed by the conversation unfolding on the screen in front of her. With thumbs moving at a rapid pace, she was mostly oblivious to everything happening in the room. As academic fellowship recipients, we had each been allowed one guest to join us for a gathering of Roothbert Fellows at a Quaker retreat center in Pennsylvania. At age sixteen, Miranda had come as the guest of her older sister—a decision she now obviously regretted. Tapping out messages with ferocious speed, she looked up only occasionally to ascertain where the discussion was headed—and whether it might soon be finished— before returning quickly to her phone.

During a break, I struck up a conversation with Miranda. "What are you doing on your phone?" I queried.

"Just, you know, texting some friends back home," she said before adding with a whisper, "These meetings are really boring, so I kinda brought my friends along."

Fascinating, I thought; she brought her friends along. We were only allowed one guest, but Miranda had found a way to subvert the rules and bring her friends with her. The irony, of course, was that her friends were geographically several hours away in Baltimore. Yet, her phone allowed Miranda to create her own social space even though her physical space was inhabited by a completely different social grouping. Faced with the prospect of being socially out of place—and she was out of place as a sixteen-year-old at a gathering of academics—she had corrected the situation by bringing her friends with her.[5]

Miranda from Baltimore, held in her hands (as do 77 percent of American teenagers) the power to do what has eluded humans for thousands of years—to transcend geographic and physical boundaries in order to communicate with others in far-flung places.[6] There she sat as a sixteen-year-old teenager, not terribly impressed with the technology—taking it for granted—but transfixed by its ability to manifest the presence of her friends among the Pennsylvania foothills.

For the majority of human existence, physical proximity has limited social relationships. Being geographically close has never forced anyone to be friends, but geographical distance has always limited with whom a person can socialize. We've always had a limited ability to practice "social selectivity" (*I choose to be friends with him, but not her*), but rejecting everyone who was geographically close usually guaranteed a lonely existence. However, social and mobile media give teenagers a heightened ability to practice selective sociality and to separate physical presence from social presence. Technology allows them to be physically present in one place, but choose to be present virtually with their closest friends who are in another location.

As technology has turned social, it has simultaneously become mobile, and it allows teenagers (like Miranda) to carve out private, personal space in public places.[7] No longer are we bound to be present wherever we are physically, or bound to be with those who are physically present with us. Rather, we manifest our own spaces, our own social group wherever we go. The result of being able to take their friends with them is that persistent social presence becomes possible for teenagers.[8] It becomes possible to always feel as if they have a group of people who are present with them.

At the same time, to the outside observer, these technologies can make teenagers appear isolationist and socially reclusive. If you've been in the church van with ten teenagers, each holding his or her own private conversations with far-flung friends via text message—while you attempt to prod them to talk to *each other* instead—then you know what I mean. Or, consider that there are at least a dozen people sitting around me as I write this in an East Nashville coffee house, but there are no audible conversations happening because we're all staring into electronic devices perched in front of us. By all appearances, we're a bunch of social recluses; but in reality we're socializing with people who are not physically proximate to us. Each of us has turned a public place into a private space. The young woman who just sat down at the table across from me looks like she is alone as she fidgets with her iPhone. But it is clear that she's communicating with a friend through some social app. Though she's not physically present with her friends, she is within reach, socially present.

## "GAMING MY FRIENDS WITH ME"

Some social technologies, such as the immersive world Second Life, have attempted to be escapist by inviting users into wholly new lives. The majority of youth have not been attracted by these technologies that provide for an alternative reality in which users are asked to create new identities and new relationships within new worlds and new spaces. Consequently, the teen version of Second Life was shuttered in 2011.[9]

However, teenagers are interested in the intersection of offline reality and online technologies that transform the boundaries of their mundane existence—especially those that allow them to maintain persistent social connection and manifest social presence with peers. This is where videogames have captured the interest of a sizable number of teenagers, especially boys.

Just as the girl with the iPhone in the East Nashville coffee shop manifest her social presence to friends in far-flung places through social apps, so teenage boys do the same thing with social games. Fully 84 percent of teen boys play videogames, compared to just 59 percent of their female counterparts, making videogames the most social of all media for boys.

Many teens socialize through multiplayer online games such as *World of Warcraft*, *League of Legends*, *Counter-Strike*, *Minecraft*, or *Roblox*. Some of these games are MMOGs (Massively Multiplayer Online Games) while others allow for just a few players, and still others are collaborative gaming or world-building environments. But in fact, nearly all games popular with teenagers—whether played on platforms such as Playstation or Xbox, handheld gaming systems, or traditional PCs—have a significant social component.

Ninety percent of boy gamers play with friends they know in person, and well more than half (59 percent) also play with online friends, leading experts to conclude that "video games play a critical role in the development and maintenance of boys' friendships."[10] Rather than giving notoriously quiet teen boys the opportunity to avoid conversations, videogames foster them. Whether gathered online, or in the same room, the vast majority of teen boys talk with friends while gaming, and 71 percent use voice connections to allow for free-flowing discussion with physically distant friends. (Interestingly, only 28 percent of teen girls who game use voice connections.)[11] The conversations include everything from strategizing about in-game play, to talking about videogames generally, to mundane chitchat—and of course a fair amount of male bravado and trash-talking.

As a result, most teen gamers report feeling closer and more connected to their friends through game play. This is especially true for boys. While 62 percent of gaming girls say they feel closer to their existing friends through gaming, a whopping 84 percent of gamer boys say the same.[12] My own middle schooler, Evan, broadcasts his *Minecraft* and *Roblox* game play to an ever-growing legion of in-person and online friends who gather to talk shop and share the mundane chitchat of life. (He'd want you to know you can find his livestream at *twitch.tv/evanbear1*). If he misses a day of gaming and streaming, he's beside himself. But it's not the games he misses (he plays a different one nearly every day), but rather the social presence of his friends.

## EVERY SPACE A SPACE FOR MY FRIENDS

Mobile technologies and social networking applications invite users to make any physical space the point of connection for their physically absent social group. It is the difference between being invited into a new world and having one's present world dramatically altered.[13] The result is that users have the power to transform every physical space into a locale for selective socialization—the practice of choosing with whom they're going to socialize, and with whom they're not. In this sense, mobile and gaming technologies are no less immersive or escapist than virtual worlds—they're simply escapist in another fashion by allowing us to transform any and every geographical space into a social environment of our making.

With a cell phone in hand, the church pew easily becomes yet another place from which teenagers can connect with their selected peer group, rather than connecting with God or the congregation that happens to be gathered with them. The hospital waiting room becomes just another place where teenagers happen to be while they "hang out" or play with friends through a gaming device. With smartphone in hand, the family dinner table becomes a place for teenagers to whisper sweet nothings via text message to significant others who are not physically present.

By throwing out the rules of time and place, mobile and social media allow for a relational persistence not otherwise easily available in a society that is always on the move. It is not the smartphone or the videogame that is irresistible, but the people on the other end. So teenagers use media to coordinate, foster, and extend social interaction beyond normal boundaries, creating a sense of presence (like Miranda) by bringing their friends with them. In an always-on-the-go society, it is these "always on" relationships of persistent presence that young people are seeking. And it is these that point to an even deeper yearning for a relational presence that is transcendent—a hunger for communion with God and others.

## EVERY SPACE A SPACE FOR MY FRIENDS— EXCEPT CHURCH

While teenagers yearn for the presence of close friends, a 2015 Pew study found that only 21 percent of teens say they spend time with their closest friend at church.[14] Without historical data and further research, it's difficult to know the full scope and meaning of such a statistic; however, it does indicate that—in the experience of most teenagers—church isn't the place you go to be with your closest friends. Certainly, we encounter teenagers who fill our youth rooms and find themselves surrounded by their closest friends, but it's likely these teens are a minority, an oddity even. For the average American teenager, it is possible that going to church entails being surrounded by vague acquaintances and distant friends.

However, what might it look like for teenagers to bring their closest friends to church in a digital age? Teenagers seek to turn every public space into a place of private gathering between them and their friends. But let's turn that around: One practice we might engage is inviting youth to bring their private friends digitally into the public space of the youth group gathering. Just as proximity doesn't create presence, so lack of proximity doesn't have to prevent presence!

One simple way to enact such a practice is through prayer requests from distant others. During a winter retreat two years ago, students were shocked when I invited them to text their friends back home and solicit prayer requests and needs. Students texted friends and family—some Christian, some not—and soon responses were pouring in. As we prayed for each person, students texted back letting their friends know that we were praying specifically for them. Suddenly, the presence of dozens of others were incorporated into the retreat.

Similarly, the presence of distant others can be brought into small groups by crowdsourcing questions through students to their friends. Through the simplicity of text messaging, it's possible to lead a small group that draws responses and interactions from a whole host of youth beyond the walls of the room.

Additionally, never allow a lack of physical presence at a group meeting to be a reason for students to be socially forgotten. Consider inviting the group to message absent members, not after group, but right in the midst of your gathering. Take time to acknowledge the value—and presence—of teenagers who are physically absent.

## BEYOND "SEE-YOU-NEXT-SUNDAY" COMMUNITY

I recently visited a church in Memphis, Tennessee, where I was surprised to see the message, "See You Next Sunday!" stenciled over the exit to their youth area. At least they were honest about their expectations, but teenage use of social media provides a powerful challenge to a church that has become accustomed to a see-you-next-Sunday approach to community. Such occasional and disconnected forms of community don't pass muster in the digital age (maybe they never should have), yet many congregations function together for an hour per week. Rightfully, teenagers are not interested in occasionally convened communities, but rather full-time intimate communities of people who are present with one another in the realities of life.

A simple practice that can function epicletically is to extend involvement with one another beyond formal gathering times. The phrase "doing life together" has become popular in some evangelical circles, but the phrase is more popular than its actuality. Extending our relational involvement beyond formal gatherings doesn't only mean that youth ministry staff should find ways to make contact with youth. Rather, we must assist youth and adults to stay involved with one another. It's one thing to have someone from the church staff or youth ministry staff reach out and make contact during the week; it's a totally different experience, however, to be involved in a community of people who are involved in caring for one another throughout the week. Such contact might in fact happen through the use of social technology, but it shouldn't be limited to this.

While the age of pastoral home visitation or church members dropping by for a visit has long since passed, it may be time to consider ways to reinvigorate these practices that seem as radical as they seem passé. What might happen if teenagers received a home visit from a youth pastor or adult volunteer? Maybe more radically, what might it look like to empower and assist youth to visit in-person with other youth from the ministry?

Of course, in a digital age, being present with one another does not necessitate in-person gatherings, and we should consider the use of social media. However, many youth ministries are in the habit of employing social media asocially. Mailing lists, message templates, and blasts of various kinds are useful for sharing information, but fail the test of presence mentioned previously. Social media practices that function epicletically will be those that invite youth and adults to care and share in personal and meaningful ways that manifest presence with one another other throughout the week. If we hope for youth to experience themselves as part of the body and *koinonia* of Christ in the world, then moving our communal interactions beyond confined meeting times is crucial. Such attempts can also function as epicletic practices that prepare our congregations and youth ministries for the transforming work of the Holy Spirit.

1. *It's Complicated*, boyd. *Why Youth (Heart) Social Network Sites*, by boyd, page 18 at *http://www. danah.org/papers/Why Youth Heart.pdf*. In addition to schools, boyd notes that home life is also a highly adult-structured environment for youth. Teenagers look for connection online because they are not allowed to go out.

2. *It's Complicated*, boyd.

3. *Why Youth (Heart) Social Network Sites*, boyd, page 21.

4. *Why Youth (Heart) Social Network Sites*, boyd, page 21.

5. Alternatively, maybe Miranda succeeded in manifesting herself or her social presence elsewhere. Though physically present with us, she was quite literally somewhere else in her mind—she was with her friends. This locale was not a single place, not secured by any particular geography, but was constructed by mental effort and through social interaction with friends geographically dispersed, and yet cognitively and emotionally connected. Whether we characterize the situation as Miranda bringing her friends with her, or whether we say she was transported somewhere else, the fact was she was not present with us—at least socially.

6. "Teens, Smartphones and Texting," by Amanda Lenhart (Pew Research Center, March 2012) at *http://www.pewinternet.org/2012/03/19/teens-smartphones-texting/*.

7. *Personal, Portable, Pedestrian: Mobile Phones in Japanese Life*, by Mizuko Ito, Daisuke Okabe, and Misa Matsuda (MIT Press, 2006); page 9. Many popular social media apps such as Instagram and WhatsApp exist only in mobile form and require the user to have a smartphone, tablet, or other mobile device to access them.

8. "Personal Relationships: On and Off the Internet," by Barry Wellman and Jeffrey Boase; page 13. Wellman and Boase have referred to this as the tendency of Internet technologies to make connection possible with "somewhat distant" people. Their point is that usually teenagers (and adults) employ social technology—not with strangers or those across the globe—but those they will soon encounter again face-to-face.

9. "Social Media and Mobile Internet Use Among Teens and Young Adults" (Pew Research Center, February 2010) at *http://www.pewinternet.org/files/old-media//Files/Reports/2010/PIP_Social_Media_ and_Young_Adults_Report_Final_with_toplines.pdf*. Only 8 percent to 10 percent of teenagers use virtual worlds.

10. "Teens, Technology and Friendships," by Lenhart, A., Smith, A., Anderson, M., Duggan, M., Perrin, A. (Pew Research Center, August 2015) at *http://www.pewinternet.org/2015/08/06/teens-technology-and-friendships/*

11. "Teens, Technology and Friendships," Lenhart, Smith, Anderson, Duggan, Perrin.

12. "Teens, Technology and Friendships," Lenhart, Smith, Anderson, Duggan, Perrin.

13. *Personal, Portable, Pedestrian*, Ito, Okabe, Matsuda, page 9.

14. "Teens, Technology and Friendships," Lenhart, Smith, Anderson, Duggan, Perrin.

*Note*: At the time of publication, all websites provided throughout this book were correct and operational.

Technology allows teens to be physically present in one place, but choose to be present virtually with their closest friends who are in another location.

# PRESENCE TEXT:

# WHY SHORT MESSAGES MEAN MORE THAN YOU THINK

*Tyler*: School is almost here.

*Logan*: Ikr

*Tyler*: Im like wait what na your lying.

*Logan*: ?

*Tyler*: When someone told me school is almost here.

*Abigail*: OK sry

*Abigail*: Bye good night:-)

*Abigail*: Hi I'm back lol

*Hannah*: Read the text that I sent Lauren.

*Abigail*: I did.

*Hannah*: We need to hangout sometime.

*Jacob*: Hey can u get on?

*Connor*: Hey I'm getting on now.

*Jacob*: U there?[1]

The idea that teenagers use social media to experience presence and to deepen relationships sounds intriguing—until you actually look at their messages. Grab a teenager's phone, peruse the messages, and you're in store for a dose of what looks like meaningless drivel. Even a quick glance at their messages and status updates would appear to confirm Nobel laureate Doris Lessing's contention that the Internet "has seduced a whole generation with its inanities."[2] The pithy nature of these messages is all but guaranteed by 140-character limits to text messages and some popular social media apps. Even still, users rarely hit the maximum message length. In America, the average text message clocks in at just 7.7 words—and that factors in the lengthy text messages of older adults who are insistent on spelling out every word![3] As emojis continue to replace words, we can expect the average text length to become even shorter.

But social meaning derives from more than the length of a message or even the specific ideas communicated. Instead of focusing on the overt meaning of messages, we need to consider how presence and relational status are communicated.

Research shows that social media largely functions for teenagers as means of "phatic communion," a function of language first documented by anthropologist Bronislaw Malinowski in the 1920's that depends relatively little on the intellectual content of the communication.[4] Phatic communion describes the "ties of union" that can be created by exchanges that appear to be meaningless—such as teenage text messages. Through repetitive, cliché, or ritualistic words and phrases, we communicate in a phatic form all the time.

A popular Budweiser beer commercial from the early 2000's characterizes phatic communication well. "Whassup?" called a group of men to one another. "Whassup?" the others replied with a guttural growl and head nod. The point was not to pass along information as much as to communicate presence: "I'm here. Do you know I'm here?" "Yes, I know you're here. Whassup?" That is the nature of phatic exchange.

Phatic exchanges create a sense of connectedness and personal availability.[5] They're "neither the result of intellectual reflection, nor do they necessarily arouse reflection in the listener," wrote Malinowski; rather, they do something far more important—they bind people together.[6] As a result, Malinowski chose not to speak of phatic communication, but rather phatic *communion*. There are obvious religious overtones in Malinowski's use of "communion," which refers to the relational intensity that can be produced by this kind of speech.[7] Far from being *less* powerful than highly intellectual or informational communication, Malinowski believed that the phatic can accomplish something our well-thought and argued statements cannot by highlighting a recognition of one another's presence.[8]

"Who are you texting?!" I asked impatiently of two distracted ninth graders, Jake and Connor, one evening at youth group. Both had pulled out their phones three times in a matter of minutes during Bible study. Jake looked at me sheepishly, "Him," he said, pointing at Connor just a few feet away.

I was confused. "What? Why? I mean, you're texting each other?" I asked incredulously. "What's so important that you needed to text each other now?"

"Just *this*," Jake snickered as he turned his phone to reveal nothing but a series of thumbs-up emojis shared between him and Connor. There must have been fifty or more, the last three shared during group. Then it dawned on me: Jake and Connor were in the process of communicating phatically, recognizing and affirming each other's presence in the group and with each other.

But why does the recognition of another's presence matter? Why is this function of the phatic so powerful? A truly phatic acknowledgement of presence is not merely an acknowledgment that the other person exists in the universe, but rather it's a declaration that the other person is *with* us, and that we are *with* him or her. The insider's language of abbreviated text-speak and emojis demonstrates belonging with one another.

Beyond the sense of belonging that derives from phatic exchanges, they also provide a sense of security that you're "with" others. Life is rough and humans do not make it very far alone, whether lost in nature or in the abyss of the eighth grade hallway. Phatic messages are a poignant reminder that social support is not far away.

Through communicating belonging and security, phatic exchanges also affirm the teenager's personal identity. Since Erik Erikson, developmental theory has affirmed that identity doesn't flow from self-definition alone but from those who declare us to be "with" them and "part" of them. So when a phatic message communicates belonging and security, it simultaneously reaffirms identity. Whether it's a phatic "whassup," a random emoji, or the vanishing Snapchat of a friend making a funny face, the true value of these constant messages is not the content but the sense of belonging, security, and identity they impart whether teens are near one another or physically separated. It turns out that in the middle of Bible study, Jake and Connor were doing far more than trading the thumbs-up emojis I could see on their phones.

In addition, utterances of phatic communion do not merely maintain a relationship, like that of Jake and Connor, but can actually create and strengthen relational bonds. In a study of couples using social media for intimate communication, a research team headed by Frank Vetere found that simple expressions such as short text messages containing commonplace phrases and words that seemed trivial to outsiders were actually "laden with emotional significance" for senders and recipients.[9] In the couples they observed, the willingness to waste time on even apparently meaningless and idle chatter "was a valuable expression of the care they shared for each other."[10] They concluded, "The regular and frequent exchanges, that have little if any informational value, are key to the strength of ongoing social binding."[11]

When teenagers communicate phatically, whatever the content of the actual words (and there may not be any discernable content at all), they are asking and answering a question of presence: "Are you here? Do you remember I am here?" And when the response comes—whatever it is—it communicates: "Yes, I'm here. I remember you're here. I am with you." Phatic exchange is a social use of language and a foundation for experiencing presence.

## INTIMACY THROUGH THE MUNDANE

Closely related to phatic exchange is the routine chitchat of teenagers, which is also criticized for its seeming lack of value. Reflecting the views of many, journalist Imre Salusinszky says that teenagers use social media for nothing more than "jabbering" and "silly inconsequential" conversation.[12] However, not everyone agrees. Kate Crawford points out that women's use of landline telephones in the 1950's was similarly dismissed as idle chatter. Yet, research showed that "intimacy over distance was sustained precisely by sharing the banalities of everyday life, by talking about what might seem to others to be insignificant details."[13]

"Insignificant details" are what critics of the micro-blogging service Twitter contend the service traffics in—and cofounder Jack Dorsey agrees. However, what critics don't understand, says Dorsey, is that the "small details in life are what connect us most."[14] Indeed, small details can connect us, and even impart a sense of intimacy, if shared on an ongoing basis. Intimacy, says theologian Kenda Dean, entails the "deeply spiritual search for another who knows what it's like to be 'me.'"[15] And many teenagers are undertaking that search by using social media to produce a constant stream of data about their lives, in the hope that if they can just share enough information, then maybe—just maybe—someone will know what it's like to be them. Through the constant stream of social and mobile media "small details and daily events cumulate over time to give a sense of the rhythms and flows of another's life" to create a sense of not merely knowing another, but being intimately present with another in the living of life.[16]

Similarly, Crawford argues that the "sharing of everyday actions, habits, and experiences—everyday 'trivia'" forges important bonds because the details that are most intimate are in fact the details that are most mundane. How so? Only a person who is truly present and involved in your life would know the little details of your life—and only someone who truly loves you would actually care.[17] Thus, sharing in chatter, participating in the everyday, can be a form of love.

In light of this, maybe it shouldn't be surprising that Jesus pointed to the Father's mundane interest in the lives of believers to highlight God's love and provision. Jesus assured his followers, "Even the hairs on your head are all counted" (Luke 12:7). God's interest in our ordinary, everyday existence is also affirmed by the Incarnation. In Christ, God takes on the fullness of human experience, and affirms that all of human life matters— not just the highs of life, but the ordinary moments as well: drawing water at the well, eating with friends, napping on a boat.[18] When we pay attention to teenagers' chatter as an expression of their humanity, we are choosing to look on them as God does.

## ATTENDING TO CHATTER AS AN ACT OF LOVE

During my first years of youth ministry, I could count on William and Michelle to invade my office after school. They'd spend hours hanging out in the youth ministry office at our church—cutting in half my afternoon productivity. Often I felt like Martha did when Jesus showed up at her house: I wanted to listen, but there was just so much to do. So most of the time, I tolerated the presence of William and Michelle, half listening to their chatter, nodding when appropriate, but being far more present to the tasks of ministry than its people. They eventually got the message that I was busy and didn't come around so much. And, to be honest, I was relieved.

When crisis hit William's life during his junior year, I tried stopping by his house and giving him a call. But he didn't want to talk about it. "It doesn't matter," he told me on the phone one day. "Don't worry about me, I'm sure you're busy."

Looking back, it's clear that my failure to attend to William's chatter was a failure to attend to the most important parts of his life: the everyday. I was ready to spring into action when a crisis hit, but in neglecting the routine details, I had inadvertently signaled that not only were they unimportant but also he was unimportant. When we parachute in during a crisis, we inadvertently tell teenagers their emergency is worth our time, but their very selves are not.

This doesn't mean that I needed to let William and Michelle take over my entire afternoon every day. Even a few minutes of daily attentive listening and talk together would have solidified my concern for their lives and their interest in mine. Boundaries are crucial and, at some point, I definitely should have said to William and Michelle: "Hey, my time is up. I need to move on to attend to some details of work," but only after being present with them in the conversation of life. By taking time to listen and give attention to the insignificant, we affirm the significance of teenagers like Michelle and William. We love and care for them in the pattern of the God who entered ordinary existence and who numbers the very hairs of their heads.

In a world of information overload, attending to the chatter of teenagers is a powerful form of pastoral care, which we haven't given nearly enough time.[19] Certainly, most youth ministries allow plenty of time to hang out, unwind, play games, and just let teenagers talk. However, there's a difference between simply providing unstructured time and attending to the chatter and unremarkable details of teenagers' lives.

## THE EPICLETIC PRACTICE OF ATTENTIVE CHATTER

There's often little time in youth ministry for true attention to the chatter and commonplace happenings in teenagers' lives. We're busy urging them to be quiet, gaining their attention, and teaching them Scripture. We're stretched thin just attending to the emergencies of teen lives, much less the everyday details. Yet if attention to the mundane reveals who loves us, then we should reconsider our priorities. Rather than cutting-edge technology, ministry with teenagers necessitates reclaiming practices that communicate our love for one another and open us for the communion-making work of the Holy Spirit. Believe it or not, giving time and attention to mundane chitchat with teenagers can be this kind of practice, one I call the epicletic practice of attentive chatter.

Being attentive involves granting teenagers our attention and thereby, our presence; being present with someone is always a matter of granting the other your attention in some form or fashion. Our attentiveness is to the chatter of teenagers, which has no apparent purpose, direction, or value. We're usually allergic to "wasting time" listening to such things, but enacted as an epicletic practice, attending to the chatter of a teenager can be a prayer for the Holy Spirit to form us into people who truly love others in the fullness of their existence.

Recently, I asked my twelve-year-old son, Evan, about why his friends who play videogames with him are some of his closest friends. "It's nice to have people who are interested in the stuff I'm interested in and who actually listen to what I have to say," Evan told me. He is looking for others who are willing to engage with him in attentive chatter. Like most adolescents, Evan chatters. A lot. That chatter is almost constantly about videogames. It would be easy for the youth pastor at our church simply to assume about Evan, "Hey, there's a kid who loves videogames," and (following the Moth Myth) to outfit the youth room with a few consoles in hopes of attracting his attention. However, while Evan does enjoy playing videogames, his deeper longing is to find belonging with a group of people who are present with him and engaged in knowing him. It will be through relationships filled with attentive chatter that Evan will become known and ultimately find belonging in the body of Christ. For this to happen, our church and youth ministry need to be a people committed to epicletic practices that lead us toward *koinonia*; game consoles are irrelevant.

There is resonance here with the concept of place-sharing described by Andrew Root in *Revisiting Relational Youth Ministry*. Yet, some have interpreted the place-sharing relationships described by Root as only occurring when we dive headlong into the suffering and tragedy of teenage lives. Entering the crises of teenagers has its place, but it's important to understand that place-sharing relationships begin, not in the tragic, the abyss, or the suffering of the teenager, but rather through place-sharing presence in the mundane, the everyday, and the decidedly undramatic.

In youth ministry, teenagers are not merely looking for someone who will share just the big moments of life, the religious moments, or the crisis moments of suffering. Generally, we have been willing to enter into all three. We show up for games and graduations. We discuss personal religious milestones and decisions with teenagers. We're there at the hospital, at the funeral, and after the breakup. But teenage use of social media reveals that teens are not looking for people to parachute into their lives on Sundays and Wednesdays, or in the big times and tough times. They're seeking relationships of knowing and intimacy built through the sharing of "a million meaningless moments."[20] They're looking for those who will be present in the little things of life: in picture comments, messages, and mundane chatter whether offline or online. It's actually these that make presence in the moments of crisis and suffering meaningful and that give entry into truly meaningful place-sharing.

Youth workers often react to hearing all this by jumping to the conclusion that it's going to require 24/7 communication with the teenagers under their care. Not so. It will certainly require a more frequent level of contact than once a week. However, frequency of exchange is somewhat less important than our attention to the mundane details of the lives of the youth under our care and the gift of presence we share with them in the moments when we do communicate. Boundaries are important; 24/7 availability is unhealthy and untenable. Rather, it is by means of setting aside space and time to be attentive that we actually come to see and know them.

All of this will sound impossible for the already overworked youth worker. Good. Because the epicletic practice of attentive chatter is not for the youth pastor or even youth ministry volunteers alone. The entire congregation should be a people of attentive chatter with one another. Teenagers need to be included in a community where attentive relationships are being fostered by all, not just by youth. The practice of paying attention to one another as we share the ordinary details of life can function as a prayer for the Holy Spirit to transform us into *koinonia*. This means that the task of relational youth ministry in a digital age is not confined to the youth meeting space, but extends into the whole congregation. This is a potentially larger view of the task of youth minister than has been traditionally conceived, but one that is necessary if our hope is for youth to experience the communion of the body of Christ, rather than merely the tight-knit sociology of a youth group.

1. These are excerpts from real text-message exchanges by youth, ages 12 to 16 in Tennessee, during the summer of 2015. Gathered and used with permission. Names have been changed.

2. "Nobel Prize Winner Lessing Warns Against Inane Internet," by Maev Kennedy, in *The Guardian*, December 8, 2007; page 20.

3. *Always On: Language in an Online and Mobile World*, by Naomi S. Baron (Oxford University Press, 2008); page 152.

4. "The Problem of Meaning in Primitive Languages," by Bronislaw Malinowski, in *The Meaning of Meaning*, by CK. Ogden and I.A. Richards (Harcourt Brace & Co., 1923).

5. "Phatic Technologies: Sustaining Sociability through Ubiquitous Computing," by Frank Vetere, Steve Howard, and M. Gibbs in First International Workshop on Social Implications of Ubiquitous Technology. ACM Conference on Human Factors in Computing Systems, CHI, 2005; see *http://www. academia.edu/364801/Phatic_Technologies_Sustaining_Sociability_Through_Ubiquitous_Computing*.

6. "The Problem of Meaning," Malinowski, in *The Meaning*, Ogden and Richards, page 334.

7. "Phatic Communion," by Gunter Senft, in *Culture and Language Use*, edited by Gunter Senft, Jan-Ola Ostman, and Jef Verschueren (John Benjamins Publishing, 2009). Later theorists (such as Roman Jakobson, "Linguistics and Poetics," in *Style in Language*, edited by T.A. Sebeok [MIT Press, 1960]; pages 350-377) expanded upon Malinowski's concept of phatic communion by talking about phatic communication as the act of keeping the channels of communication open by establishing and maintaining communication. However, Senft points out that these two concepts, while related, are not identical. According to Senft, what Malinowski meant in employing the term *communion* was not keeping communication lines open but truly using speech to achieve a binding rapport that he intentionally called communion.

8. "These Foolish Things: On Intimacy and Insignificance in Mobile Media," in *Mobile Technologies: From Telecommunications to Media*, edited by Gerard Goggin and Larissa Hjorth (Routledge, 2009); page 256.

9. "Phatic Technologies," Vetere, Howard, and Gibbs at *http://www.academia.edu/364801/Phatic_ Technologies_Sustaining_Sociability_Through_Ubiquitous_Computing*.

10. "Phatic Technologies," Vetere, Howard, and Gibbs at *http://www.academia.edu/364801/Phatic_ Technologies_Sustaining_Sociability_Through_Ubiquitous_Computing*.

11. "Phatic Technologies," Vetere, Howard, and Gibbs at *http://www.academia.edu/364801/Phatic_ Technologies_Sustaining_Sociability_Through_Ubiquitous_Computing*; Also, "Mediating Intimacy: Designing Technologies to Support Strong-Tie Relationships," by Frank Vetere and Howard Gibbs, First International Workshop on Social Implications of Ubiquitous Technology. ACM Conference on Human Factors in Computing Systems, CHI, 2005. Also, "New Media, Networking and Phatic Culture," by Vincent Miller, in *Convergence*, Vol. 14, No. 4, November, 2008; pages 387-400. Vincent Miller argues that phatic technologies are on the rise precisely because they can keep youth from wasting time by allowing them to engage in noninvasive communication, effectively maintaining relational presence with intimate friends while simultaneously engaging in the rest of life.

12. Imre Salusinsky quoted in "These Foolish Things," in *Mobile Technologies*, Crawford, page 254.

13. "These Foolish Things," in *Mobile Technologies*, Crawford, page 255.

14. "These Foolish Things," in *Mobile Technologies*, Crawford, page 258.

15. *Practicing Passion: Youth and the Quest for a Passionate Church*, by Kenda Creasy Dean (Eerdmans, 2004); page 129.

16. "These Foolish Things," in *Mobile Technologies*, Crawford, page 259.

17. "These Foolish Things," in *Mobile Technologies*, Crawford, page 252.

18. I am indebted to theologian Christy Lang Hearlson for calling my attention to the ways in which the Incarnation is an affirmation of the mundane aspects of human existence.

19. The idea of sharing the mundane as caregiving is suggested by Crawford.

20. I'm indebted to Mark and Susan DeVries for this phrase, which they use to describe the way that intimacy within marriage is built on a daily basis.

# THE GREAT SHIFT:

# YOUTH AND THE RISE OF NETWORKED INDIVIDUALISM

"Our answer to all these devices and apps is simple," a veteran youth worker told me recently. "We have a basket at the entrance to the youth room, and we ask students to deposit their devices on the way in. No muss, no fuss. Problem solved." He's not alone. Whether cubbies, bins, or baskets, the practice of creating technology-free spaces is widely employed in youth ministry. Similarly, the practice of limiting student use of technology during trips and events has a long history in youth ministry going back at least to the invention of the Sony Walkman in the 1980's. Whatever the method, the underlying assumption is that if we pry the technology from the fingers of teenagers, then everything will be fine. They'll be able to focus on relationships with people around them. They'll be able to be attentive to the message and Scripture for the day.

If the Moth Myth is all about adding technology to youth ministry to be relevant, then this, the Basket Myth, is the reverse: We assume that good youth ministry can happen when teenagers are physically separated from their phones. We assume that the only thing that has changed in culture is the increase of devices, and if we can wage war against devices, then everything will be fine.

But what if the devices aren't the problem? What if the devices are just an indicator of a larger cultural shift, a change that doesn't disappear when the battery dies or the phone is placed in the basket? As we discussed in the first three chapters, we have not paid attention to why teenagers are using social media. However, we also have not paid careful attention to the shift in the social operating system of American culture that has accompanied the rise of devices. Sociologists, such as the eminent Manuel Castells, have been declaring for well over a decade that the Western world is undergoing a massive shift in the structure and style of social relationships. A new system of relationality is emerging. It is partially driven by social technology, and it is partially driving the desire for social technology. Either way, what is being called networked individualism is quickly becoming "the dominant form of sociability in our age," which means this shift is changing teenagers' understanding and expectations of what it means to be in relationship with others.[1] In reality, the shift to networked individualism is affecting all of us. Your basket isn't going to stop it.

## BEYOND THE BASKET

It's not enough to understand how teens are employing social media; ministering to teens in the digital age also requires understanding shifts in the social milieu that are occurring alongside the rise of social media. Some of these shifts we'll be able to embrace, but many run counter to the ideals of Christian *koinonia*. As a result, youth ministry needs more than a basket in which to place devices. We need to offer an alternative to the dominant social operating system. *Koinonia* is presented by the apostle Paul as exactly that—an alternative form of relationality by which Christians are called to live. In the second half of this book, we'll explore a biblical and theological model of *koinonia* and its potential for shaping youth ministry (and Christian communities broadly) in an age of networks. But before we can offer an alternative, we must clearly understand the social system of networked individualism. We must understand where it came from, what it demands of teenagers (and all of us), and how shifts in relational expectations affect teenagers and the lives they lead. Only when we understand the water in which we swim, can we adequately compare and contrast the Christian operating system of *koinonia*, and have any idea how we might move youth ministry into nourishing our call to a different kind of communal experience.

## THE NETWORK: A NEW SOCIAL LOGIC

There was a time when the language of the network was confined to computer geeks, but today we are increasingly living in what has been described as networked culture. The network has become the dominant cultural logic, shaping our thinking about a variety of domains.[2] Amidst this shift to network thinking, "our economy, public sphere, culture, even our subjectivity are mutating rapidly," writes Kazys Varnelis.[3]

One of these mutating domains is that of human relationships, an area in which we are starting to see one another less as confidants and more as connections, or more properly "network nodes" to whom we are connected.[4] Therefore, to say we are living in a networked culture does not describe merely the *technology* we use, but in fact the very social *configuration* of our culture: We have moved from traditional "communities" of family, villages, and voluntary associations to "personalized communities embodied in me-centered networks," writes Castells.[5] Today, the image of individuals being contained within bounded, hierarchically organized, discrete groups (think tribes, churches, towns, clubs) to which we belong "one group at a time" is largely an image of the past and does not adequately describe what we find on the ground.[6] Rather, according to sociologist Barry Wellman, a shift to networked individualism is liberating people from the restrictions of tight-knit groups and freeing them to form personal networks that are large, loosely knit, and which give expanded opportunities for learning, problem-solving, and relational interaction.[7] Effectively, in contemporary society we're able to experience community without having a community. To understand that statement, we have to parse what community means.

## Community in a Networked World: Space or Feeling?

The tendency in sociology has been to define *community* by reference to bounded physical spaces (neighborhoods, churches, and so on). However, relationships today are pursued without the restrictions of space and time (as a result of fast transportation and asynchronous communication technologies), and so limiting the definition of *community* to particular spaces does not describe the full scope of the relationships in which people are actually involved.[8] Therefore, rather than defining *community* "as group-like neighborhoods and villages" says Wellman, "it is more useful to define *community* as networks of interpersonal ties that provide sociability, support, information, a sense of belonging, and social identity."[9]

Community does not disappear, but becomes defined as a sense or feeling of social support, rather than a group to which we belong.[10] This is a helpful distinction, for it allows us to move towards defining *community* in terms of the quality of an experienced phenomena rather than merely proclaiming any interactions among people in close geographical proximity as "community."

This shift—from groups of community to networks through which community is experienced—has been supported by a variety of social and technological changes, says Wellman, everything from divorce laws to birth control, from suburbanization to air transportation.[11] Each of these shifts (and many others) have allowed for individuals to become unbounded from local, homogeneous, and tightly-knit forms of belonging and community.

## Personalized Community

We personalize everything in contemporary society from the coffee we drink at Starbucks, to the computers we use, even to the relationships we have. We are no longer bound to place-based connections where we socialize with others who are convened together in the same place (neighborhoods, churches, and so on) and who necessarily know one another. Relationships are now purely person-to-person, and the fact that we share space with others is increasingly irrelevant in determining sociability as social technologies permit selective socializing without concern for geography.

At this point, you may be looking around saying: "Wellman is out to lunch. Groups haven't disappeared! I see groups everywhere." And you'd be right, of course, groups of people still get together. Wellman's point, however, is that our relationship to the groups has changed. Teenagers are no longer set in a particular group, nor derive their primary identity from one group. Rather they have relationships with individuals whom they encounter through various groups; and rather than relating most closely to a group, their relationships are set within a network that is "diffuse and sparsely knit—with vague, overlapping, social, spatial boundaries [as] many of the people they deal with do not know one another."[12]

Rachel illustrates well the reality of the new networked sociality. She's in the tenth grade and on the varsity cheer squad in her rural Tennessee high school. She makes good grades, is active in student activities, possesses a bubbly personality, and is known by absolutely everyone in her small school. At lunch she sits among a group of girls who huddle together daily at the same lunch table, having staked out a spot in the cafeteria midway between what they describe as the "majorly popular people" and the "awkward" side of the room. Many of these girls have known one another since kindergarten; a few of them have parents who even grew up together in their small farming town. By all appearances, Rachel is a member of a tight-knit community indistinguishable from the kind of relationships her parents experienced in the same high school cafeteria. But spending just a little more time with Rachel reveals this isn't quite the case.

"We're not all friends really, as much as, you know, like we just sorta eat lunch together. It's hard to explain," Rachel told me as we walked toward her fifth-period class. When I pressed for an explanation, and who Rachel counts as her close friends—the people that truly support her—she names a motley crew of individuals: One of the girls from the lunch table. Two friends from her church located twenty minutes up the road. Another friend from the church she used to attend in the next town over. A girl she sees at summer camp each year and keeps in touch with via social media. She names only one girl on the cheerleading team as her friend. "It's something I do, but I wouldn't say most of those girls are like, my 'friend' friends," Rachel says. It turns out that many of the people Rachel names as part of her inner circle don't even know one another, or only know of one another vaguely. They all know Rachel, of course, but her close friends are what sociologists would call sparsely-knit. Rachel's life weaves in and out of a variety of different groups—student council, cheerleading, church, family—but her social support and identity are not derived from these groups, per se, but from the individuals that she weaves together into her personal network.

As teenagers like Rachel float between a variety of groups, they encounter individuals to add to their personalized networks, individuals who may not even know one another. And social and mobile media allow them to keep in touch with those individuals across distances like never before. The community that teenagers like Rachel experience doesn't arise from a tight-knit group, rather it's an experience derived from a collection of people whom the teenager assembles into a personal network of friends and acquaintances.

Rachel's experience is not entirely new; culture has been trending toward networks of this nature for some time. But ultimately, social media have taken the place they have in contemporary society—and the lives of teenagers—because they effectively fill the requirements of the already burgeoning societal shift toward networked individualism. Social media provide teenagers the tools for building these networks and maintaining their viability. Teenagers are *not* becoming networked individuals primarily because they use social media; rather, teenagers employ social technology because it allows them to live more successfully as networked individuals in an already networked society.

## TRACING THE RISE OF NETWORKED INDIVIDUALISM

To more fully understand the social world in which youth are coming of age and the way they use the technological tools afforded to them, it's helpful to trace the slow shift from previous forms of sociability toward networked individualism. Wellman argues that this is a shift that began with the Industrial Revolution as large-scale changes in transportation, communication, and work enabled a move away from localized community toward what he calls place-to-place community.[13]

## Localized Community: Door-to-Door Relationships

Prior to the Industrial Revolution, social relationships were generally bounded by geography and kinship in ethnic groups, villages, or neighborhoods.[14] In any given physical settlement most people knew one another, and their relationships were limited by how far their feet could take them. People experienced broad-based social support because everyone in the village knew everybody else.

As with any social configuration, door-to-door society placed demands upon individuals. It demanded that they reside in a particular location; moving to another village or neighborhood meant the slow withering of old social connections and the need to establish new ones in the new location.[15] Door-to-door society also demanded conformity to communal expectations. Fail to conform to social norms, and one could easily find oneself shunned by the entire tight-knit community.

## Convened Community: The Place-to-Place Shift

With the advent of fast transportation (rail, auto, and then airplane) and near-instantaneous communication technologies (telegraph and telephone), we saw a change from localized community to place-to-place community. These technologies made it possible to live in one place, but to have significant relationships in another place. I call this "convened community," because the hallmark feature is people from different places convening together in community.

The decline of the neighborhood church and the rise of regional church (and eventually the mega church) is one visible result of the shift from localized to convened community. By the middle of the twentieth century, it became possible for a family to get in the family car, leave their neighborhood of residence without speaking to any neighbors, attend church miles away where they interacted with others who had arrived from other locations, and then get back into their vehicle and return home.

In convened forms of community, attendance is the critical marker of community rather than kinship or geography.[16] A physical space for social interaction is still necessary—whether home, church, or community center—but the boundaries of the community are defined by who physically "shows up" to the place of meeting and who does not. Community comes to be based upon *attendance* at a place, rather than *attending to* one another. The quality and nature of the relationships between members are not of much concern. In fact, since convened community happens at specified times and places, relationships become occasional and sporadic.

The place-to-place model still defines how many of us in youth ministry think about community. We count the youth who *show up* to youth group as committed students. If people attend church by showing up at a meeting space at an agreed upon time, then they're considered active members of the community. Leaving such a community is a matter of deciding not to show up, or showing up at the meetings of a different community somewhere else. Because, after all, what is demanded of individuals if they hope to experience community is simply this: showing up.

## Toward Personalized Community

Wellman argues that we are now moving beyond convened community as the dominant form of social structure and toward a "person-to-person" connectivity that he calls networked individualism. In this form of sociality, it is the "I-alone" that is the agent and portal of social connection, says Wellman. Phone numbers no longer call places, they call individuals. Addresses no longer are fixed in space, but deliver letters (e-mail) directly to individuals. And "youth group" no longer identifies a group of people bound to one another, but rather a place where teenagers might—or might not—find a few friends to add to their network. The physical space that the "I" occupies is completely incidental because "supportive convoys travel ethereally with each person."[17]

What makes networked individualism truly individual is that the makeup of these "supportive convoys" is completely up to the discretion—and the effort—of the individual. "Community" is no longer a given, but it must be created, convened, and maintained by each individual in the form of a network. And each person's network is unique. While there may be overlap, no two networks are the same. Youth are able to personalize their own "nebulous, far-flung, and sparsely-knit, but real and supportive communities."[18]

## SMALL GROUPS IN A NETWORKED WORLD

Our middle school guys' small group was falling apart. With seven regulars and a rotating cast of three or four others, the group really couldn't get any bigger. It also couldn't get any more disconnected. These guys didn't know one another, and further, they didn't care to. It wasn't that they were from different schools, or had dramatically different interests, it was simply that their networks didn't overlap. In nearly twenty years of youth ministry, I'd seen blank stares and bored faces before, but this time around I could tell there was another dynamic at work: They weren't quietly surviving the curriculum; they were trying to survive one another.

In an age of networked individualism, getting youth in the same room doesn't mean you've created a group or any sense of community. It only means you have a cluster of teenagers engaged in selective sociality and the building of personalized networks of friends.

If you're finding it increasingly difficult to get groups of youth to congeal and find a sense of community together, you may be experiencing the effects of networked individualism. A sense of belonging and an experience of community does not arise for networked individuals simply by being rubber-banded together by the title of a group. You can get them to come up with a group name and invent a group cheer. You can have them memorize the youth ministry mission statement. You can put them in matching T-shirts, and you can give them the same adult leader each week—but don't expect those actions to create a significant experience of community and belonging. Rather than seeing themselves as part of a group, networked individuals are more likely to use the group as a hub "to find a few friends." This was basically the situation with our group of middle school guys—only worse. They weren't even using the group to find a few friends; they were enduring the hour until they could whip out their phones and reconnect with the myriad of friends they already had in their individual lives.

When we couldn't get groups to gel, we'd often just try harder to create a group identity, but what we actually needed was to foster individual relationships in the group setting. We ultimately determined that what our middle school boys needed was to recapture the ancient Christian practice of the holy kiss. Yes, you read that right. Middle school boys may think of a different kind of kissing, but I'm suggesting that in a networked world we need to engage them in the *epicletic practice of the holy kiss.*

## HOLY KISSES IN A NETWORKED WORLD

Theologian Jürgen Moltmann notes that every expression of love comes with its own body language and that there is literally a "body language" that flows from a group of people experiencing the love of God together. The laying on of hands and the washing of feet are examples, but historically, the most intimate form of a Christian "body language of love" was the holy kiss or the kiss of peace.

I'm not advocating for reinstating the literal practice of the kiss, but recapturing the social function, personal meaning, and openness to God and others. Contrary to Greco-Roman social custom, the kiss was exchanged on the lips to demonstrate the family intimacy of Christians. The kiss functioned phatically, too, affirming one's presence and belonging in the family of God. But the most significant aspect of the kiss of peace was its exchange between each member and all the others. It wasn't a single kiss exchanged between the congregation and the leader upfront; rather *each individual was embraced, one-at-a-time, by every other individual.*

As we move toward a theological exploration of Christian *koinonia*, this becomes an important point to remember: *Koinonia* is not one-on-one. *Koinonia* does not consist merely of two people in relationship; rather, *koinonia* is constituted from three or more people who are *each in individual* relationships with one another, and yet bound together by their mutual relationality. Thus, as an expression of *koinonia*, the kiss of peace is not a group exercise, nor is it a group hug. It is an individual practice, carried out in a one-on-one relationship that is in turn situated within (and cannot be separated from) the relationships of the larger body of Christ. In a group hug it doesn't matter who the person next to you is, you're all just hugging one another and saying, "We're all part of the group." The identity of the individuals making up the "we" hardly matters. But in *koinonia* the individual is recognized, identified, and valued by every other individual, and in turn these individuals are recognized and valued by all the others. *Koinonia*, then, stands in stark contrast to the sparse-knit nature of personalized community, as well as the anonymous groups of place-to-place community.

For our middle school guys, turning to the epicletic practice of the holy kiss means they don't need some kind of pseudo-group identity. They don't need a team cheer, group T-shirts, or a small group name. They don't need a cohesive group experience, whether backpacking, whitewater rafting, or playing team-building games. There's nothing wrong with any of those things, they're just not enough. Rather, we needed to help them engage in individual relationships—one to another—so that the experience of the group was built from the overlapping, individual relationships they had with one another. Fostering such relationships certainly has a psychological and sociological effect, but we began cultivating these prayerfully in recognition that it is the Holy Spirit who would ultimately bind them together as brothers who share in Christ.

We started simple, with the holy exchange—not of a kiss—but an emoji. It happened one night when one of the guys asked to use the restroom, and then proceeded to prank a friend in the group with repeated "thumbs-up" emojis. His friend's phone started going berserk in the middle of discussion but, instead of confiscating the phone, I invited—actually demanded—that they all get their phones out and text bomb the guy in the restroom. The victim shared his friend's number, and we blew up his phone with hundreds of texts. When he returned to the meeting room, we all had a good laugh and then continued with the discussion.

At the end of the evening, taking my cue from the texting prank, I again had them whip out their phones and trade numbers. I assigned them the task of texting one another—every guy in the group—sometime during the week. Most of them didn't even have one anothers' numbers. One out-to-lunch seventh grader didn't even know the names of several of the other guys in the group! My instructions were: "Send just a thumbs-up emoji—something more if you want—but just the emoji is fine to let that person know you're praying for him that day." I gave them an additional task of texting the emoji again an hour before our next group meeting to remind one another of our gathering.

Of course, this sounds ridiculously simplistic. And it was. Yet, every week we upped the ante on their individual involvement with each of the other group members. Some weeks they were assigned just one other person in the group to pray for and text during the week. Some group nights we'd allow a few minutes for them to pair up as partners to talk and pray together. Every week we kept up the practice of emoji exchanges.

Together, these practices became our form of the kiss of peace with middle school boys, by engaging them in individual exchanges of love, set within the broader context of the group. Surely, there's more we could have done or expected. Our practices fell so short of the early church practice of a holy kiss that it's embarrassing—except for the fact that this is the nature of all epicletic practices. They all fall short of approaching what our prayer for transformation is. Even during the Lord's Supper, the epicletic prayer is almost embarrassing as the celebrant prays for the Holy Spirit to make our gifts of bread and wine to be the body of Christ. Really? We offer ordinary bread and wine? And yet this is, of course, Christian tradition following the command of Christ. Likewise, my prayer each week was that the Holy Spirit would take emojis traded by middle school boys and transform them into a kiss of peace. Our prayer, enacted in a practice, was that the Holy Spirit would transform their relationships with a bond of love and make them brothers together and sharers in Christ.

I'm not certain what the epicletic practice of the kiss of peace might look like in your ministry context. I hope that it can take the form of more meaningful relational exchange than where we started with my middle school guys. But maybe not. What makes such a practice epicletic is not the intensity of the experience, but the way in which the practice functions as a sincere prayer for the Holy Spirit's transforming power. When we invite youth to come together and to affirm, care for, and embrace one another as individuals in the context of the group, we begin to build relational bonds that are meaningful. At the same time they act as scaffolding for the Holy Spirit to transform these relationships together into something more—the *koinonia* of Christ.

1. *The Internet Galaxy: Reflections on the Internet, Business, and Society*, by Manuel Castells (Oxford University Press, 2003); pages 130-131.

2. "The Meaning of Network Culture," by Kazys Varnelis, in *Eurozine*, January 14, 2010. See *http://www. eurozine. com/articles/2010 01-14-varnelisen.*

3. "The Meaning of Network Culture," Varnelis.

4. "Social Isolation in America," by Miller McPherson, Lynn Smith-Lovin, and Matthew Brashears, in *American Sociological Review* (71, 2008); pages 353-375. See *http://www.washingtonpost.com/wp-dyn/content/article/2006/06/22/AR2006062201763.html.* Just half of Americans report they have a friend they consider a confidant—a figure that is 22 percentage points lower than thirty years ago.

5. *The Internet Galaxy*, Castells, pages 128-29.

6. *Networks in the Global Village: Life in Contemporary Communities*, by Barry Wellman (Westview Press, 1999).

7. *Networked*, Rainie and Wellman (MIT Press, 2012).

8. *Networks in the Global Village*, Wellman, page 18.

9. "The Networked Nature of Community: Online and Offline," by Barry Wellman, Jeffrey Boase, and Wenhong Chen in *IT and Society* (Summer 2002); page 154. Also, see *http://www.academia.edu/2983698/The_networked_nature_of_community_Online_and_offline*. Wellman et al. are not arguing that neighborhood (geographically local) relationships no longer exist; rather, they comprise only a small percentage of a person's larger social network. See also "Personal Relationships: On and Off the Internet," by Jeffrey Boase and Barry Wellman, in *The Cambridge Handbook of Personal Relationships*, (Cambridge University Press, 2006); pages 709-723.

10. "The Networked Nature of Community," Wellman et al, page 154.

11. "The Networked Nature of Community," Wellman et al, page 158.

12. "The Networked Nature of Community," Wellman et al, page 160.

13. "The Networked Nature of Community," Wellman et al, page 152. Wellman et al. particularly highlight changes to transportation and communication, though not disregarding the rise of capitalism, bureaucratization, industrialization, and urbanization.

14. "Physical Place and Cyberplace," by Barry Wellman, page 232. See *http://groups.chass.utoronto.ca/netlab/wp-content/uploads/2012/05/Physical-Place-and-Cyber-Place-The-Rise-of-Personalized-Networking.pdf.*

15. While written correspondence might have allowed for the maintenance of social ties, this technology was inaccessible to the large number of people who were illiterate or without the financial resources to send written letters.

16. Some have described this kind of community as voluntary association; for example, see *Democracy in America*, by Alexis de Tocqueville (1835).

17. "The Networked Nature of Community," Wellman et al, page 160.

18. *Networks in the Global Village*, Wellman, page 37.

*Note*: At the time of publication, all websites provided throughout this book were correct and operational.

Teenagers are not becoming networked individuals primarily because they use social media; rather, teenagers employ social technology because it allows them to live more successfully as networked individuals in an already networked society.

# DIGITAL DEMANDS:

## WHAT NETWORKED INDIVIDUALISM REQUIRES OF YOUTH

All is not well in the brave new world of networked individualism. Teenagers are coming of age in a world that "confers social and economic advantages to those who behave effectively as networked individuals."[1] But behaving as a networked individual—meeting the demands of this new social operating system—is not without drawbacks.

As with any social system, networked individualism demands that its inhabitants behave in certain ways in order to be socially successful. Those who lived in the era of door-to-door community had to conform to social expectations or face being shunned by the village. Those who lived in the era of place-to-place community had to attend group meetings, services, and functions, or face being cut off from community. And when we consider networked individualism, we find four demands placed upon teenagers. Meeting these demands can have negative effects.[2]

# DEMAND #1: CREATE A PERSONAL NETWORK

True to its name, networked individualism requires an individual to establish a unique set of personal relationships (what sociologists call an *egocentric network*) from which she receives care and support. This is how Rachel, the rural Tennessee teenager we met in Chapter 4, experiences community. She doesn't find her identity and community in any one group; rather she's at the center of a network of friends and acquaintances who are connected directly to her. Her friends from church are part of her network, but not everyone who attends youth group is part of Rachel's network. A few girls from the lunch table are part of her network, but not all of them. In the networked world, joining a preexisting group doesn't guarantee meaningful community. So either youth, like Rachel, successfully build a network through their own effort, or they are likely to face some level of relational isolation. Building a network involves finding friends from across a variety of social groups and then keeping those connections open. For close connections, Rachel communicates daily, or even more often, whether through in-person encounters, text messages, or social apps. She is sure to keep tabs on her close friends' social media posts so she can comment on them and demonstrate their importance to her. For more distant connections, Rachel occasionally "likes" a picture, or messages a friend to see what's up. The point is, building a network takes work. If Rachel doesn't expend the relational work necessary to keep her network connections healthy, then she will ultimately lose them and her network of social support—a fearful prospect in the age of networked individualism.

The burden to craft a personal network and the possibility of losing one's network community can ultimately mire young people in fear and anxiety. If you've seen a teenager panic when separated from his phone, then you've witnessed the struggle of being out of touch with friends. However, you've also witnessed the fear of permanently losing network members by being temporarily out of touch.

The church is called to embody *koinonia*, an alternative operating system that delivers teenagers from the fear induced by networked individualism. The demand to create an egocentric network differs significantly from the communion of the church, in which youth are called, drawn, and invited into the cloud of witnesses and the body of Christ. In *koinonia*, belonging does not depend on personal effort.

In Chapter 8, we'll more fully explore how communion counters the anxiety induced by network individualism, and we'll suggest epicletic practices that can prepare your youth ministry for transformation by the communion-making power of the Holy Spirit.

## DEMAND #2: KEEP THE NETWORK ENGAGED

Building an egocentric network is not a one-time endeavor. It is necessary to keep the network alive by making oneself engaging, interesting, and attractive, lest your network audience lose interest and slip away. Maintaining the interest and attention of the network as audience can be difficult thus, in a networked world, *"impression management* is key to developing a social identity."[3] Getting likes is a competitive venture, and having just the right pictures, status updates, videos, tweets, and texts is paramount.

Like many teenage girls, Rachel is a master at curating her online image to maximize likes and minimize embarrassment. Rachel admits to agonizing over status updates and fudging on her likes/dislikes when filling out profiles; she is keenly aware of what's going to be interesting and sound cool to the members of her network. When her family visited Disney World last year, she was sure to post pictures and updates endlessly, hoping to attract likes, while keeping her network members engaged and interested in what she was doing. But when her youth pastor tagged her in an unflattering photo on Facebook, Rachel quickly removed the tag in hopes that her network members wouldn't notice.

Rachel knows how to strike the right pose for group shots; she's hyper aware of getting just the right knee bend, hand-to-hip placement, and tilt of the head in order to produce the best possible outcome. Reports show that the average woman takes seven selfies for every one that she posts, and Rachel is no exception.[4] In fact, seven seems a little low to her. "It totally depends on the day," she says with a laugh. Social media are incredibly well-suited for the task of impression management, and while Rachel uses Instagram because that's where her friends are, she's also thankful for the built-in photo filters that allow her to tweak and edit her photos on the spot.

All of this is impression management at work, and it's driven by the need to maintain the interest of one's network members. But beneath all of the perfectly chosen words and poses, there are aspects to Rachel's self that she keeps carefully hidden. The self that she presents online is shined and buffed and staged and produced to be consumed by her network members. Ultimately, there's a difference between presenting the self and being the self, and the demand that teenagers engage their network audience leads them to hide the self rather than reveal the true self.

Communion, as an alternative social operating system, can release individuals to be themselves, as they find acceptance and love as sharers in Christ and not based upon their own efforts. In Chapter 9, we'll explore how communion counters the hidden self. We'll also suggest epicletic practices that, through the power of the Holy Spirit, open young people to being themselves rather than staging themselves for their network.

## DEMAND #3: GROW THE NETWORK LARGE

Having a few friends is not enough for the social system of networked individualism; rather "those with relatively big and diverse networks, including many weak-tie associates, gain special advantages" and are more likely to get the help, support, or information they need.[5] Of course, maintaining close relationships with a large number of people is difficult. And that's OK, because networked individualism doesn't demand close relationships—it merely demands that you have connections with a variety of people. In fact many partial relationships are considered far better than a few tight ones in a networked world.[6] For example, having a large number of people who fill the relational role of "audience member" can collectively become an important resource when you need "the wisdom of crowds."[7] Barry Wellman and Lee Rainie declare that, in a society of networked individualism, those with "broad-ranging networks are often in better social shape and have a greater capacity to solve problems than those who have smaller networks. Quantity *does* equal quality."[8]

Social media are well-suited for helping teenagers like Rachel grow a vast network of partial relationships. With over six hundred friends on her Facebook account alone, Rachel is unable to keep in touch with all of them, but she is able to drop birthday messages to important friends and leave occasional likes on the posts of others in her network. Like others, when she needs the help or resource of a particular friend, that person is just a message away. Despite their longing to escape from partial and transitory relationships, the demand to grow the network pulls teenagers away from the presence and intimacy they desire. Instead, they find themselves in faceless relationships where they are not deeply known.

In contrast, the experience of *koinonia* leads us to declare one another to be brothers and sisters, as we engage in relationships of presence and knowing. Yet, instead of being a community of presence, church is often one of the most anonymous communities that teenagers encounter all week. In Chapter 7, we'll explore the faceless and partial relationships that pervade networked individualism, and we'll suggest epicletic practices that can function as prayers for the Holy Spirit to transform us into communion rather than a mere collection of people.

## DEMAND #4: BE SOCIALLY SELECTIVE

Even though it's necessary to maintain a large network of weak ties, networked individuals must be selective about the individuals on whom they spend their limited time and energy. "Tune your network by dropping people who don't seem worth spending attention on regularly," Internet guru Howard Rheingold advises his readers.[9] This kind of cutthroat social selection is necessary or else networked individuals may find themselves with a large social network filled with people incapable of actually giving them the support and help they need.

When nasty rumors began to fly around school about her close friend Michelle, Rachel was torn but ultimately decided it was best to keep her distance. "She's kinda made her decision," she told me, "I don't want to get dragged into that." While Rachel didn't cut off all connection to Michelle, it wasn't socially expedient for Rachel to spend much time on the relationship—and so she didn't.

That's how things work in the world of networked individualism but, in the communion of Christ, the worthless and uninteresting are not unfriended. Rather, they are the ones we are called to "honor the most" (1 Corinthians 12:23). In the communion of Christ, teenagers are meant to receive love and belonging when they have no social value, and they in return are invited to give love without considering the social value of others. In Chapter 10, we'll further explore the selective sociality of networked individualism, and we'll suggest epicletic practices that can help our ministries become places in which people are valued equally regardless of social standing.

## TURNING OUR ATTENTION TO COMMUNION

In the first three chapters, we discovered that American adolescents are hungering for relationships characterized by presence and intimacy. Yet, as we've learned in this chapter, their search is increasingly pressured by the demands of networked individualism. Fulfilling these demands often puts teenagers at odds with their desire for meaningful relationships. Building, growing, and engaging a large network of partial connections leads youth toward anxious, weak, and instrumental relationships— something far less than the relationality for which they have been created and for which they long. Networked individualism leaves youth hungry for relationships of presence, but there is a better way.

It's time to turn our attention from the experience of teenagers, and the social system of the culture around us, and fix our full attention on God's intended social-operating system for the church. As we've said previously, the way forward in youth ministry will not be discovered by focusing on technology, but rather by focusing on the proper nature of Christian *koinonia*. In an age of networked individualism, youth ministry cannot be content to offer better technology, but instead we must offer teenagers entry into a community that is powered by a completely different engine and logic. That's precisely how the apostle Paul presents the idea of *koinonia* in First Corinthians, as a countercultural social system distinct from the surrounding world.

To understand how *koinonia* differs from networked individualism, it's necessary to momentarily leave the twenty-first century and consider how Paul's theology of *koinonia* contrasted what was happening in the first century. You might be surprised to learn that our world and Paul's are not so far apart.

1. *Networked*, Rainie and Wellman, page 256.
2. For an exploration of the potential benefits of networked individualism, see *Networked* by Rainie and Wellman.
3. *Why Youth (Heart) Social Network Sites*, boyd, page 21. See *http://www.danah.org/papers/WhyYouthHeart.pdf.*
4. "This is How Much Time We Spend Taking Selfies Each Week," by Sarah Coughlin, in *Refinery29*, April 24, 2015. See *http://www.refinery29.com/2015/04/86241/women-selfies-average-statistics.*
5. *Networked*, Rainie and Wellman, page 263. See also *http://networked.pewinternet.org/2012/10/18/how-to-thrive-in-a-networked-world-book-chapter-excerpt/.*
6. *Networked*, Rainie and Wellman, page 41.
7. *Networked*, Rainie and Wellman. See also *http://networked.pewinternet.org/2012/10/18/how-to-thrive-in-a-networked-world-book-chapter-excerpt/.*
8. *Networked*, Rainie and Wellman. See also *http://networked.pewinternet.org/2012/10/18/how-to-thrive-in-a-networked-world-book-chapter-excerpt/.*
9. *Net Smart: How to Thrive Online*, by Howard Rheingold (MIT Press, 2014); page 229.

*Note*: At the time of publication, all websites provided throughout this book were correct and operational.

Despite their longing to escape from partial and transitory relationships, the demand to grow the network pulls teenagers away from the presence and intimacy they desire. Instead, they find themselves in faceless relationships where they are not deeply known.

# BEING COMMUNION:

## CORINTH AND THE ALTERNATIVE OPERATING SYSTEM OF KOINONIA

The youth ministry of Saint Peter and Paul Orthodox Church in Philadelphia, Pennsylvania, looks different from what you might expect. When Father Stephen Siniari's duties at the church are over, when the divine liturgy has been performed, and he has presented his congregation with the blood and body of Christ in the Eucharist, he takes off his robes, puts on blue jeans and a dirty baseball hat, and hits the streets looking for her. He's looking for a fifteen-year-old runaway from Cherry Grove, New Jersey. It has been years, and despite the fact that he's never turned up even a trace of her, he keeps searching.

Siniari has printed business cards with a phone number on them, and he goes with members of his congregation to the most dangerous neighborhoods in Philadelphia, Camden, and Atlantic City looking for her. They ask the people they encounter to call the number if they happen to see the young runaway. Often the people Siniari encounters agree to help him look. But not always. He and his congregants have been beaten, mugged, and robbed—all while looking for the runaway. It's a high cost, but they can't give up looking. And so they keep going, and they keep handing out the cards.

Every few days Father Stephen's phone rings—the phone that is designated for the search. And usually the caller says, "You know, I haven't seen the girl you're looking for, but—um—I'm missing. I ran away, and I'm wondering if you can help me get back home." And he does.

You see, the fifteen-year-old runaway that Father Stephen is looking for doesn't actually exist. It's just a story he tells to find the people for whom he's looking—usually young runaways, both girls and boys, who too soon find themselves trapped in prostitution or drug trafficking by pimps and human traffickers.

Father Stephen's youth ministry, and that of his church members who hit the streets with him, is to rescue teenagers from the streets and reunite them with their families. It's their passion.

When I heard Father Stephen speak about his experiences, I had difficulty putting together two disparate images: First there's the streetwise rescuer on Fridays and Saturdays who navigates the underground culture of sex traffickers and teen runaways. The other image is that of stoic priest chanting ancient prayers and blessing bread and wine in ancient ritual on Sunday. These two worlds seemed totally incongruous to me, and so I brazenly asked him, "Do you ever feel a disconnect, like you're living two lives, one in blue jeans rescuing runaways and one in robes presiding at the Eucharist?"

"Disconnect? Disconnect?" Father Stephen was surprised by the question and responded: "No, I feel precisely the opposite because in the Orthodox Church, we don't just serve communion; we *are* communion. What we do in the liturgy informs how we live toward one another and the world. What we do on the streets is a direct result of being communion together."

I struggled to understand what he meant. For most Christians, Communion refers to a ritual meal that we eat together. In your church it may happen every quarter, month, or week. We talk about celebrating Communion. Partaking in Communion. Receiving Communion. Serving Communion. But it's not normal for us to talk about *being* communion.

But Father Stephen is right. Long before Communion was reduced to wafers and sample-sized cups of juice, it described the kind of communal interactions engaged in by the followers of Jesus. The meal, the Lord's Supper, was one of the things that the people who were communion engaged in together; the meal itself wasn't Communion. Luke tells us that after Pentecost believers "devoted themselves to the apostles' teaching, to the community [*koinonia*], to their shared meals, and to their prayers" (Acts 2:42). Luke's use of the Greek *koinonia* can be translated into English as fellowship, sharing, or communion. But it's difficult for us to understand the full force of what he's talking about because we've reduced "Communion" to a ritual meal, "fellowship" to youth events with messy games, and "sharing" to something we do with photos and little else. For early Christians, *koinonia* was the social operating system that determined how they lived and interacted with one another—and how they ministered to the world around them. That's the tradition behind Father's Stephen's understanding of communion. It describes the social operating system of his church body, their way of relating to one another, and their ministry and witness in the world.

In Chapter 4, we surveyed networked individualism, the emerging social operating system of our era, and we explored two previous social operating systems: door-to-door and place-to-place sociality. But these are not the only possible forms of sociality that exist. Just as Father Stephen supposed, communion (*koinonia*) is meant to describe the social operating system of the church. Many of our churches don't have a clue about this—but that's not just a modern problem. A close read of First Corinthians reveals that the church in Corinth was also comfortable serving the Lord's Supper, but had difficulty understanding Communion as anything more than a meal of remembrance.

In 1 Corinthians 10–12, Paul tells the Corinthian believers that *koinonia* isn't a meal we eat, but is a way of approaching others and the world that challenges the normal human ways of social operation. Just as *koinonia* challenged the Roman Empire's approach to sociality, it also challenges many aspects of networked individualism today.

## TROUBLE IN CORINTH

Paul is very clear in 1 Corinthians 11 that there is trouble in Corinth. And his wording is blunt: "When you meet together as a church, I hear that there are divisions among you" (verse 18)—when you come together, you're actually being torn apart![1] What divisions? Are they divided by their theology or politics? No. Rather, Paul chides, "So when you get together in one place, it isn't to eat the Lord's meal. Each of you goes ahead and eats a private meal. One person goes hungry while another is drunk" (verses 20-21).[2] This is the only place in the New Testament where the term the *Lord's Supper* appears, and Paul doesn't use it to give the meal a name, but to contrast the Lord's Supper with their "private meal."[3] He's saying that because of the divisions among them, they are not eating the Lord's Supper, but their own meal, eaten according to their own social customs of competition and exclusion!

## COMPETITIVE EATING IN CORINTH

Today if we want intrigue, competition, bravado, and backstabbing, we tune in to reality television; in the Roman Empire, people just went to dinner. Both the Roman dinner feast (*convivium*) and the drinking party that followed were fierce opportunities to gain and display social status. These meals were magnificent performances of social stratification and an opportunity to display, in a rather visible fashion, the nature of one's social network in a "status-conscious, honor-centered society."[4] The significance of these banquets extended far beyond the dinner hour and encapsulated "the aspirations and aims of the culture as a whole."[5]

The host of the supper, reclined in the place of honor, would assemble a cadre of friends and relations, seating those of greatest social standing closest to him. Meanwhile, those with least standing might not even be seated in the same room, since seating would flow out into the courtyard.[6] Those with higher status would receive choice food and prompt service;

those of lesser status might be served poorer food or merely leftovers.[7] If you wanted to flaunt your VIP status, it was even possible to secure an invitation to arrive early and enjoy the festivities before "ordinary" guests arrived. In addition, "games of honor and humiliation were played out in conversation," with some people not permitted to speak and others not spoken to.[8]

Often the meal would include a religious eating or drinking ritual dedicated to an idol. Despite the religious veneer, the real purpose was to ritually establish social and economic connections between participants by making them *koinonoi* (partners) together in the idol. But being "partners" didn't make the dinner any less cutthroat. Indeed, the social competition, bullying, and brutality played out today through social media may seem tame by comparison. Historian Susan Alcock summarizes it well:

> *All in all, a convivium could be (for some) a pleasant, convivial occasion; for others, the dinner party from hell. In essence, this is all about dinner as hierarchy, as rule making, dinner as creating social alliance and distance, dinner as a diacritical feast.*[9]

The meal was a microcosm of the Roman Empire's dominant social operating system—a competitive, stratified system of honor and shame in which individuals jockeyed to distinguish themselves at the expense of others. Similar in some ways to the emerging system of networked individualism, this is the social system that Paul was interested in challenging with a theology of Christian *koinonia*.

## COMMUNION BEYOND CONNECTIONS

Just as banquets and ritual meals devoted to pagan idols were opportunities to see a microcosm of the Roman Empire's social system at work, so Paul imagined that the Lord's Supper meal should function in the same way—a tangible demonstration of what it meant for the church to be the *koinonia* of Christ. But that wasn't happening in Corinth and so, in First Corinthians, Paul carefully lays out the meaning of Christian communion in contrast to the social norms of Corinth.

While the Corinthians were accustomed to establishing useful connections and camaraderie at pagan banquets, in 1 Corinthians 10, Paul describes the relationships of Christian *koinonia* in a way that likely left them speechless. "Isn't the cup of blessing that we bless a sharing (*koinonia*) in the blood of Christ?" Paul asks. "Isn't the loaf of bread that we break, a sharing (*koinonia*) in the body of Christ? Since there is one loaf of bread, we who are many are one body, because we all share the one loaf of bread" (1 Corinthians 10:16-17).[10]

It sounds simple enough, right? But the significance of Paul's statement that the cup we bless and the bread we break is *koinonia* in the blood and body of Christ is easily lost on modern readers. The ancient (and especially Jewish) understanding was that the life was in the blood, and so *koinonia* in the blood of Christ is to share in the very "life-principle" and living existence of Christ.[11] This kind of intimacy with God was unfathomable by worshippers who never got closer to God than watching a priest pour blood on an altar.[12] Thus, the significance of drinking Christ's blood and eating Christ's body—sharing and becoming one with the very essence, identity, and existence of Christ—simply cannot be overstated. Paul is saying that as Christians we share in the very essence and life force of Christ: His life becomes our life, his body becomes our body. Believers do not merely affiliate with Christ or pledge allegiance to Christ, but rather our individual lives become inextricably entwined with Christ. The life within you is *Christ's* life within you. As such, the depth of *koinonia* in Christ is unparalleled.

But that's just the beginning. The *koinonia* believers have with Christ is certainly startling but, in 1 Corinthians 10:17, Paul reveals an even more startling aspect: All those who partake of the blood and body of Christ also find this *koinonia* with one another; partaking in fellowship with Christ necessarily transforms our relationships with all the rest who are in fellowship with Christ.[13] If we eat the bread, our lives are intertwined with Christ, but also "since there is one loaf of bread, we who are many are one body"—our lives are to become intertwined with one another in exactly the same way.[14] Translated as literally as possible, Paul is saying, "Since one bread, one body the many are."[15] We become Christ's body together by eating Christ's body, or as the old adage says, "You are what you eat."[16] Christians *become* the one body they share, and sharing (*koinonia*) in

Christ makes them partners, sharers—one—with all others who share in Christ.[17] While we do not lose our individuality, we nevertheless cannot be understood any longer as mere individuals.[18] But neither are we a collective or mere assembly, rather we are a communion best described as the body of Christ. This is a form of sharing far beyond the kind of casual and surface-level sharing to which we are accustomed, but, biblical scholars agree that *this* is the climax of Paul's argument: The crucified and risen Christ, with whom we find unity, becomes the source and cause of our unity, the *koinonia* of the body of Christ.[19]

What we've just learned from Paul's words would have certainly disturbed the Corinthians. Remember, this was a society driven by social distinctions. Jockeying for social position, outdoing one another, attempting to attract attention, were all deeply ingrained in the way that Corinthian society worked. The Corinthian Christians might have been able to shrug off Paul's statements in Chapter 10 about sharing deeply in one another's lives, but he doesn't let them off the hook. He continues on in 1 Corinthians 11–12 to explore the implications of this *koinonia* for the way that the Corinthian Christians live together. Because of the depth and nature of their fellowship in the blood and body of Christ, this communion of people must relate to one another and to those outside the *koinonia* far differently than was customary in a culture given to self-focused connections and competitive sociability. Fellowship in Christ isn't just a nice idea. Paul says it should change how they operate.

## HANDING OVER THE SELF

In his attempts to disabuse them of the notion that the gathering of the church should look anything like the self-seeking social gatherings of the surrounding culture, Paul paints a vivid picture of the nature of Christian *koinonia* in contrast to the customary form of social connections. And he begins with a story. "On the night on which he was betrayed, the Lord Jesus took bread" (verse 23b). Paul knew that starting a banquet with a memorable story about the host was a custom among the Corinthians. Functioning as the ancient equivalent of a much-liked Instagram or status update, banquet hosts would decorate the dining area with images of their great accomplishments, or tell stories about their past victories.[20] Paul upholds that tradition even as he radically subverts it: He tells a story about the host of the Christian meal; but this story is rooted in the host's self-sacrifice instead of self-aggrandizement. The story of the Last Supper is a story about Jesus giving his body for the sake of others. Paul doesn't tell the story simply for the sake of remembrance; he has another purpose. Remember, he's just told the Corinthian believers that they are sharers together in the very life principle of this Jesus. They are in fact the "one body" of him who gave his body for others. Consequently, if they are the body of Christ, their proper posture is self-giving love on behalf of others. This completely contradicted the social traditions of Corinth (as well as today's system of networked individualism) in which making a name for oneself, forging beneficial connections, and displaying one's value were highly prized and pursued.

## FAILING TO DISCERN THE BODY

Immediately after retelling the story of the Last Supper, Paul warns the Corinthians about eating the meal in an unworthy manner, and he says that those who eat without "discerning the body" (verse 29, NRSV) bring judgment on themselves. This is not an instruction about how to handle the bread, but how to live together in community. Remember, Paul has already told them that all who eat of Christ form "one body" (10:17). Thus, it is not the bread as body, but the church as body that Paul wishes the Corinthians to discern—specifically that "all belong equally to one another."[21] This is crucial because failure to fully discern and recognize the gathered church as the body of Christ is the very reason for their divisions. The Corinthian church was comprised of individuals from across the social spectrum, some wealthy and powerful, some impoverished and powerless. These class distinctions were being played out in the way that the Corinthian Christians ate the meal together—and the way they lived their lives together.[22] They were failing to discern that they were the body. Privatized and individualized faith was on display in Corinth, and rather than relating together as the body of Christ, they had become but a collection of believers connected by little more than their common interest in self-forged relationships and social standings. Discerning the body is not a matter of table manners or social pleasantries, but a matter of recognizing our communion in Christ, which destroys all social hierarchies.

The key to discerning the body of Christ is self-examination, says Paul.[23] Examination is Paul's shorthand way of addressing "how well one's life relates to Christ and how well one's love ties one to others, who, though many, are one body in Christ."[24] The Corinthians were accustomed to their social gatherings being an opportunity to promote the self, not examine it. But Paul is presenting the gathering of the church for the Lord's Supper as the opportunity to practice a new form of social relationship characterized by radical concern for others without personal attempts to establish one's status.[25] He who eats unworthily is the one who proclaims the new covenant and order of reality, and yet in the same moment acts and lives according to the old order of social hierarchies and self-aggrandizement.[26] The call to examination of the self in the meal functions as a sort of system-wide reboot, reorienting them again to the social operating system of communion characterized by self-giving love and care for others.

If the church is going to function as communion for young people in networked society, then self-examination of the ways in which our actions (inside and outside the church) unwittingly contribute to personal gain and self-aggrandizement, is vital and necessary. All of us, teenagers and adults, need a regular system reboot that helps us recall our identity as the *koinonia* and body of Christ, and to realign our ways of relating together. The discernment of the body of Christ does not lead to social niceties, manners, or genteel hospitality, but to social transformation—ways of living together and loving one another that contrast with the connective behavior of life under the demands of networked individualism.[27] Through practices of self-examination, we come to recognize that all, "rich and poor, are joined together in Christ, share equally in his blessings, and should be treated worthily."[28]

## GIFTS FOR THE BODY

In addition to importing their competitive dining practices from the surrounding culture, the Corinthians were trying to show off their gifts and abilities to further their social standing. It was normal fare at any religious banquet for guests to gain prestige by putting their apparent spiritual powers on display through exuberant acts of tongues speaking or prophecy. Add ample wine to a bunch of attention-seeking Corinthians anxious to display their spiritual powers in the midst of communal worship, and Paul's admonition that worship should be "with dignity and in proper order" (1 Corinthians 14:40) makes considerably more sense.

Paul recognizes the diversity of gifts and abilities of the Corinthian believers, but he completely reframes their meaning and use. "It is the same God who activates all of them in everyone," he says, and each is a "manifestation of the Spirit" (verses 6-7, NRSV). In pointing to the activity of God as the source of these gifts, Paul makes it difficult for the Corinthian believers to personally boast in them. Then he takes things a step further by redefining the very purpose of these gifts. Though doled out to individuals "just as the Spirit chooses" (verse 11, NRSV), these gifts are not given to individuals so that they can find status or honor, but rather they are given "for the common good" (verse 7, NRSV).[29]

Here the body becomes Paul's infographic for understanding the nature and meaning of communion in relationship to gifts and diversity.[30] God's gifting of the members of the body is not a sign of God's favor on certain individuals, nor is it intended for the establishing of a social hierarchy in the church. Rather, "God has so arranged the body . . . that there may be no dissension within the body, but the members may have the same care for one another"(1 Corinthians 12:24b-25, NRSV). In communion, gifts are given for the good of the body, not for you as an individual. Though communion should be diverse, for the strength of the body, that diversity should not lead to social hierarchies. And while low status was reason for exclusion (or lesser treatment) in the social economy of Corinth, the exact opposite is true in the body of Christ, according to Paul. "On the contrary, the members of the body that seem to be weaker are indispensable," Paul writes in 1 Corinthians 12:22 (NRSV). Each member has been arranged by God, and has a vital function in the body—they cannot be excluded— and those that seem socially dispensable should actually receive greater honor in the *koinonia* of the body of Christ.

All of this surely would have been as mind-bending for Paul's Corinthian readers as it is for Christian believers today who are increasingly accustomed to the instrumental relationships of networked individualism.

# COMMUNION IN A WORLD OF CONNECTIONS

The image of the body of Christ formed by *koinonia* with Christ that emerges in First Corinthians stands in stark contrast to both the ancient Corinthian social operating system and our own emerging system of networked individualism.

We learn from Paul that Christian communion is not some sort of fuzzy feeling, social extroversion set into overdrive, or human ritual that unites people in the sociological ritual of dining together. Rather, communion is the work of the Holy Spirit incorporating us into the body of Christ, such that we become one with Christ and with one another. Communion is expressed in social equality, selfless self-giving, diverse unity, and the pouring out of our gifts and selves in care and love for others while following the pattern set by Christ who handed himself over. (These aspects of Christian *koinonia* form the groundwork for the practices that we will explore in Chapters 7–10 as ways of responding to networked individualism.)

All of this demands an entirely countercultural way of structuring social relations, in which relationships are ordered not by their perceived social value but by the fact that all parties in the relationship have been invited to the table by Christ. Paul does not just want the church at Corinth to treat one another with respect, nor even to view themselves as connected or linked, but rather to recognize themselves as vitally bonded and knit together through drinking the life-blood of Christ. As a communion, they now share in the life-blood of all members of the body of Christ. Their present circumstances and futures are vitally linked together.

While networked individuals are the hub and center of their networks as they try to attract enough diverse connections to give them security and social support, the body of Christ functions as the Spirit arranges it, drawing us together across class, status, color, and backgrounds. In fact, the selective sociality of the Corinthians not only operated counter to this recognition, but also it was damaging the diverse and multivariant Spirit-ordered body.

When churches are merely networks for finding a few friends, we fail to discern the body of Christ. When churches organize in such ways that certain colors, income levels, orientations, or ages find themselves in the courtyard outside and eating meal leftovers, then we grieve the Spirit and sabotage the church's oneness that testifies to the truth of the gospel. It is through the diversity of gifts and individual composition that the communion of Jesus is configured to care well for one another as it announces and shows forth God's healing to the world.

Like us, the Corinthians were used to using social gatherings as opportunities to display their value, status, and desirability. They even developed customs and technologies for their mealtime gatherings that promoted this.[31] Contemporary teenagers, savvy in the mores of networked individualism, similarly use social and mobile technologies as vehicles to display their value, status, and social desirability. They are pushed to gain attention, keep attention, and grow a large network of acquaintances while using others as instrumental nodes in the anxious work of personal network building.

Paul's concern was that the church in Corinth "was beginning to resemble the dominant imperial society to which it was supposedly God's alternative."[32] Similarly, the church today can either discern the places where Christian communion stands at odds with networked individualism, or we can simply adopt networked individualism as the inescapable "social operating system" of our era and configure the church as an organization that capitalizes on the desires and needs of networked individuals. The latter may plead "relevancy," but it will ultimately fall short of God's calling—and the needs and longings of young people in search of lasting identity, community, belonging, and presence.

1. *First Corinthians*, by Joseph Fitzmyer (Yale University Press, 2008); page 433. The phrase e΄pi« to\ aujto in 1 Corinthians 11:20 that gives rise to the common English translation "together" can be understood as a spatial reference but also to indicate unity of purpose and sharing.
2. See 1 Corinthians 11:20-21. Self-concern seems to be at the heart of each person going ahead and eating what each person brought for her or himself. Whether this was a matter of people bringing their own supper, or as some commentators contend, a matter of those of lesser status receiving the leftovers and dregs, the result is the same: The "have-nots" (what Paul literally calls them in verse 22) are treated poorly and go hungry. However, argues Paul, the neglect of those who are poor would not persist if this were the Lord's Supper. There is a connection here, then, between social justice and equality and the communion of the body of Christ. We see this in Acts 2 as the believers share everything in common and distribute to any who had need. The responsibility of the Christian communion to care for the needs of others is revisited in Acts 6 where the Grecian widows were being overlooked in the daily distribution of food. There we find a helpful reminder that the desire

and commitment to caring for the "have-nots" (again as Paul calls them) does not always find perfect structural execution, and the disciples consequently put structures and systems in place to ensure that the Christian communion lives appropriately in its care for one another. Delegation, structures, and systems—even technology—then can be helpful to the body of Christ in living out its calling to be communion in the world. It is important to make a distinction between the desire for communion and the execution of living as communion in the world. We see this again in 1 Corinthians 11. Paul criticizes not only their intentions, which should be focused on eliminating divisions, but he also gives them sound practical advice which will help them live more fully into the intentions properly formed. For example, he ends his direct discussion of the Lord's Supper telling them to "wait for each other" (11:33) when eating, and if they are hungry, to eat at home before coming together for the Lord's Supper.

3. *First Corinthians*, Fitzmyer, pages 429 and 434. In Greek, kuriako\n dei√pnon. While there is certainly nothing wrong with referring to this meal as the Lord's Supper, we should recognize that there is neither anything prescriptive here in Paul's writing, and no clear indication that this is the proper name by which early Christians referred to the meal (if, in fact, there was a proper name at all). The name of the meal as *eucharistia* is first recorded toward the end of the first century in the *Didache*, and Fitzmyer notes that the name Eucharist derives from Paul's use of eujcaristh/saß (thanksgiving) in verse 24.

4. *1-2 Corinthians: The New Cambridge Bible Commentary*, by Craig Keener (Cambridge University Press, 2005); pages 96-97.

5. *1-2 Corinthians*, Keener, pages 96-97.

6. If you can imagine an overhead visual of such a gathering, it would not look dissimilar to a picture of an egocentric social network today, with the convener at the center and radiating lines of social connections moving out from him.

7. *Conflict and Community in Corinth: A Socio-Rhetorical Commentary on 1 and 2 Corinthians*, by Ben Witherington (Eerdmans, 1995); page 241. "It was the normal practice to rank one's guests in terms of social status, with those of higher status eating with the host in the dining room and others eating elsewhere and getting poorer food."

8. "Power Lunches in the Eastern Roman Empire," by Susan E. Alcock, in *Michigan Quarterly Review*, Vol. XLII, No. 4, Fall 2003; pages 591-606.

9. "Power Lunches," Alcock, pages 591-606.

10. *First Corinthians*, Fitzmyer, pages 390, 439. Most modern translators tend to render *koinonia* in this passage as "sharing" or "participation," though the King James Version shaped four hundred years of Christian tradition in the English-speaking world by using the word *communion*. *Koinonia* here can mean "participation" in the blood and body of Christ. Also, as a result of the KJV's translation of *koinonia* as "communion," the word "has come to signify sharing in the eucharist" and has consequently been reduced to a meal.

11. *First Corinthians*, Fitzmyer, page 390.

12. *1 Corinthians*, by Richard Horsley (Abingdon Press, 1998); page 140. We should not assume that Christian initiation happened through partaking in the Lord's Supper; Richard Horsley says that while "the Corinthian believers had become part of the body through baptism, the sharing in the cup and bread was a renewal of their solidarity in Christ." See also *1 Corinthians: A Commentary on the First Epistle to the Corinthians*, by Hans Conzelmann (Fortress Press, 1988); page 171. According to Hans Conzelmann, some commentators see the meaning here that the cup is the "means to the acquiring of communion." Others emphasize that "the eating of the one bread creates participation in the body of the Lord" and "their joint partaking of it confirms the Christians to be members of the body."

13. *1 Corinthians*, Conzelmann, page 171. The blood indicated here is shorthand for the salvific death of Christ, thus the "communion of the blood of Christ" can be understood to mean communion

(*koinonia*, participation) in the death of Christ and the self-giving of Christ. See also *First Corinthians*, Fitzmyer, page 391. Fitzmyer observes that Paul's placement of the verb e˙stin at the end of the phrase about the body of Christ (oujci« koinwni÷a touv sw¿matoß touv Cristouv e˙stin) contrasts with his placement in the initial phrase about the blood of Christ, indicating a desire on Paul's part to make a stronger connection between communion and body in the latter part of the verse: "To\poth/rion thvß eujlogi÷aß o§ eujlogouvmen, oujci« koinwni÷a e˙sti«n touv ai°matoß touv Cristouv; to\n a‡rton o§n klw◊men, oujci« koinwni÷a touv sw¿matoß touv Cristouv e˙stin." See also *1 Corinthians*, Conzelmann, page 172. Conzelmann agrees that Paul is making an intentional link between the eating of Christ's meal and participation in Christ's body. He notes that the reversal of bread and cup here from its normal liturgical order (an order that Paul shows us he is well aware of in Chapter 11) has significance in that Paul's structuring of this passage "is aiming at an interpretation of the community by means of the Lord's Supper. . . . This link between the Lord's Supper and the concept of the church is the new element which he introduces into the understanding of the sacrament."

14. In this instance, the King James Version best captures the abrupt transition of thought between verses 16 and 17 in 1 Corinthians 10: "The cup of blessing which we bless, is it not the communion of the blood of Christ? The bread which we break, is it not the communion of the body of Christ? For we being many are one bread, and one body: for we are all partakers of that one bread."

15. Author's translation of o¢ti ei–ß a‡rtoß, e≠n sw◊ma oi° polloi÷ e˙smen in 1 Corinthians 10:17.

16. *1 Corinthians: Anchor Bible*, by William Orr and James Walther (Doubleday, 1976). Orr and Walther refer to this as *Christosomatosis*.

17. The reference to the body of Christ in verse 17, says Conzelmann (*1 Corinthians*, page 172), is "not meant figuratively": The church is the body of Christ. koinwni÷a touv sw¿matoß touv Cristouv (participation in the body of Christ) makes them koinwnoi« (partners, verse 18).

18. *First Corinthians*, Fitzmyer, page 392: "Bread is a form of food for life, and so our common sharing in the oneness of that sustenance brings about a union of all Christians in and through the life of Christ himself."

19. "The Body of Christ," Wedderburn, page 76. See also *First Corinthians*, Fitzmyer, page 391.

20. "Power Lunches," Alcock. See more on the role of stories and images in Roman banquets.

21. From *The New Interpreter's Bible*, by J. Paul Sampley, Vol. X (Abingdon Press, 2002); page 939.

22. "Social Stratification in the Corinthian Community: A Contribution to the Sociology of Early Hellenistic Christianity," by Gerd Theissen in *The Social Setting of Pauline Christianity* (Fortress Press, 1982); pages 69-119. See http://www.academia.edu/11926411/Social_Stratification_of_the_First_Century_Corinthian_Christ-Association_A_Systematic_Review. Gerd Theissen has convincingly argued against the older view that early Christians, particularly those at Corinth, were uniformly poor. Depending on textual clues Theissen's sociological study indicates that at least some members came from the upper strata of society while the majority were from the lower social strata. Today, Theissen's view has been widely accepted and explains in part the schismata of which Paul speaks in the letter. See also *Conflict and Community*, Ben Witherington, page 246. Similarly, Witherington recalls that prominent members of the Corinthian church included Erastus, the Corinthian director of public works (Romans 16:23) and that Gaius had a home large enough to host Paul and the entire gathering (1 Corinthians 16:15 and 1:16), so there is good evidence that at least some members among the Corinthian believers possessed significant status and wealth within the city.

23. *The New Interpreter's Bible*, Vol X, page 936.

24. *The New Interpreter's Bible*, Vol X, page 939. "So, proper discerning of the body is at once an assessing not only of one's relation to Christ but also of one's relation to all the other members of the body. Ultimately, these two facets of discerning the body are not separable because the believers are so directly and fully associated with Christ and with one another in Christ." While I learned from an early age that receiving the Lord's Supper should be preceded by a time of personal confession to

God for sin, I was never led to understand this as a time to examine one's life in relation to the body of Christ, and the attitudes and behaviors toward the body. Yet, Conzelmann says that by the time of the writing of the *Didache* (mid-to-late first century C.E.), the command for examination of "one's attitude" rather than "one's inner state" is institutionalized by requiring both "confession of sins and reconciliation with one's enemies before the Eucharist" (*1 Corinthians*, Conzelmann, page 202). There could be a connection here to the kind of examination that Jesus urges in Matthew 5:23-24, in which he says to leave your gift at the altar and "go and be reconciled to your brother" before continuing with the offering. Nevertheless, the examination that Paul calls members to is a self-examination. It does not happen with others, or by others, but appears to occur privately. "Proper assessment of one's self, and self-correction if need be, is pre-requisite to worthy eating and drinking in the Lord's supper" (*The New Interpreter's Bible*, page 937). The recognition that you are a member of the body of Christ, that you are not your own, and that the Lord's Supper is not yours even if you have purchased the elements, is at the heart of the examination and discernment to which Paul calls believers in 1 Corinthians 11. We do not eat for ourselves out of our own provisions, rather we eat of Christ's body—we eat what Christ has handed over to us, and we are all members of Christ's body, so we eat of the provision of one another.

25. *First Corinthians*, Fitzmyer, page 435.

26. *First Corinthians*, Fitzmyer, page 435. Fitzmyer understands the examination as a matter of letting "each one scrutinize whether he rightly understands what remembrance of the Lord, his Supper, and his death actually mean and whether one is disposed to proclaim them by such eucharistic reception."

27. *First Corinthians*, Fitzmyer, page 448.

28. *1 Corinthians*, by David E. Garland (Baker Academic, 2003); page 551. Additionally, in *1-2 Corinthians*, by Keener, page 99, the author notes, "By treating members according to worldly status rather than God's perspective, they were dishonoring Christ's own body."

29. See 1 Corinthians 12:7 (NRSV). Paul will repeat this refrain again several times in upcoming chapters, including 14:12 and 14:26.

30. Though I refer to the "body" as Paul's infographic, and his use of the concept bears striking similarity to a popular metaphor in Greek and Roman literature, it must nevertheless be pointed out that for Paul these are not mere words but truth. See also *Paul, the Stoics, and the Body of Christ*, by Michelle Lee, (Cambridge University Press, 2008); pages 126-127.

31. For a discussion of the various customs and inventions designed to allow banquet participants to display their value, status, and desirability, see *From Symposium to Eucharist: The Banquet in the Early Christian World*, by Dennis Smith (Minneapolis: Fortress Press, 2009).

32. *1 Corinthians*, Horsley, page 164.

*Note*: At the time of publication, all websites provided throughout this book were correct and operational.

All of us need a regular system reboot that helps us recall our identity as the koinonia and body of Christ, and to realign our ways of relating together.

# COMMUNITIES OF THE FACE:

## FINDING FULL PRESENCE IN A WORLD OF PARTIAL RELATIONSHIPS

Daisy wasn't lonely, but she was alone. Halfway through ninth grade at her southern Idaho high school, she was well known among her peers as the angry fat girl with a foul mouth. Somewhere along the way, maybe in elementary or middle school, Daisy had learned to push back against the names and taunts: fatty, tub of lard, whale. She'd heard them all, and she'd learned that throwing back expletive-laced comments of her own could shut up the name-callers for a while. Eventually, she learned she could avoid the comments altogether by striking first. By the time she reached high school, she was quick-witted, sharp-tongued—and she was mean. Daisy was ready to criticize any victim she encountered—if for no other reason than to keep herself from being the subject of jokes and taunts. Though she was naturally quiet, it didn't take much egging to cause Daisy to go on a rant about the jocks, cheerleaders, teachers, or anyone else who crossed her path. Most people wouldn't have pegged Daisy as lonely.

Though she had alienated many of them, and frightened others, she still had plenty of peers to sit with at lunch and talk to in the hall. Daisy knew everybody, and everybody knew Daisy. She'd learned to put up a good façade, but her relationships were faceless in the sense that few people knew the real Daisy and what she endured at home. Daisy didn't have friends who were truly present in her life, or who truly knew her. Though unorthodox and brash, she was meeting the demands of networked individualism and building her own egocentric network filled with connections. Still, Daisy was alone—known by so many at school and yet faceless at the same time.

## FACELESS CULTURE

Networked individualism creates the urgency to construct a large network of hundreds or thousands of relationships. Rather than surrounding the self with a set of close, comprehensive relationships as might exist in a tight-knit group, network proponents argue that the way to be well-resourced with social support in the network age is to pursue a multitude of boutique relationships. Each of these partial relationships meets only a few relational needs, but together they provide more social support than a small, bounded community ever could.[1] The trade-off is that the partial, boutique relationality of networked individualism becomes a *faceless* relationality.[2] With too many relationships to be known well by many (or any!) of them, networked individuals are prone to interact with others as faceless objects to manipulate, or worse yet, as depersonalized obstacles to maneuver around.[3]

Theologian David Ford calls the self that is produced by such an arrangement the "faceless self" because people are encountered by others as if they are faceless others without human individuality.[4] If you have ever taken a ride on the New York City subway, seated just inches from another human being but without having any kind of meaningful interaction or even eye contact, then you understand the meaning of a faceless face-to-face world as people become merely objects with which we interact (or simply ignore). It is not just subway interactions that are affected by the faceless face-to-face culture in which we live; even many of our closest relationships are reduced to mechanized, faceless interactions.

In an early research interview, Melissa, a student from a youth group I'd led some years prior, derailed my planned interview questions and wanted to talk instead about the recent separation of her parents. After a lengthy conversation, the discussion finally turned toward my topic of online community.

"Technology gives a larger community and an opportunity for a different level of that," Melissa told me.

"Different level?" I asked. "As in deeper? more shallow? or just different?"

"Depends," Melissa said, "but look at us now. I haven't seen you in how long and here we are having an actual conversation, as opposed to if I actually saw you around and was like, 'Hey, what's up? Well, nice life. Catch ya later.'"[5]

Her comment pierced me to the core because I could remember numerous Sunday mornings and Wednesday evenings when our interactions closely resembled that quick and trivial form of pre-programmed, almost robotic dialogue, "Hey, what's up? Well, nice life. Catch ya later."

As Christians, we too often operate in the same faceless manner as the rest of society. On Sunday mornings we crowd people into a room, face them forward, and at some point during the worship service we engage in "thirty seconds of friendliness." In some churches this takes a liturgical form: "The peace of Christ be with you." In others it is more casual: "Good morning, how are you?" Rarely does it deviate from being a brief interlude before returning to our face-forward seating positions, closed-off from one another. The "turn and greet one another" portion of the typical American worship service often feels awkward and unfulfilling, because it highlights the faceless relationships and weak ties that members of our congregations have with one another.

To be clear, networked individualism doesn't create a faceless society, it simply perpetuates and extends this reality. We have lived in an increasingly faceless society for generations. In the past thirty years, studies show that, while our total number of "friendships" has increased, the number of people we count as close confidants has plummeted.

Today, nearly half of Americans say they have just one person with whom they discuss important matters.[6]

Similarly, when we look at teenagers specifically, today's teens report lower levels of loneliness than thirty years ago, and more teens say they have people they can talk to than ever before. But when researchers ask contemporary adolescents if they have a friend who will help them if needed, the numbers slump when compared to the past.[7] Teenagers have saturated their social networks with hundreds of relationships, but the vast majority of these relationships are partial or cursory connections. Teenagers have friends who will talk to them, but far fewer who will stand by them.

While the promise of networked individualism is to allow individuals to create their own community wherever they are, the reality is that networked individualism leaves young people searching for intimacy amidst a sea of technology. Teenagers might feel less lonely because of the sheer amount of socializing, but that doesn't necessarily translate into being present with one another in real and meaningful ways. Students like Daisy don't necessarily feel lonely, but they find themselves in faceless relationships in which they interact with others without truly being cared for or known. That's not the experience of loneliness, but the experience of being alone.

We believe humans were created for face-to-face intimacy through which we know one another deeply as persons, and in which we express love and material care for one another. Social interaction that is meaningful "faces" one another as we share our essence and experiences with one another. The evidence of truly "facing" the other is care and love for the other that is expressed in action. This is what Paul was getting at in warning the Corinthians to discern the body of Christ. If they discerned the body of Christ, then they would express that through actions that cared for and valued one another. David Ford describes the proper form of our relationality as both "facing" the other and "being faced"—phrases by which he means to describe, not bodily postures, but the intimacy of knowing and being known as a person in a relationship of loving care.[8] This is not merely God's intention for us individually, but also another way to describe the church as *koinonia* is a "community of the face."[9]

Indeed, while youth ministry has been occupied with determining how to best use Facebook, the more pressing matter is determining how to be a community of the face with and for young people like Daisy.

## TURNING TO THE TRINITY

How might we determine what *koinonia*, or as Ford calls it, a community of the face, looks like in our time? This is a difficult problem. Fellowship will certainly look different depending on the context, so it's important to focus on the essential qualities of Christian fellowship, not its temporal and culturally bound expressions.[10] Discerning the essence of *koinonia* relationships is especially important in a digital age in which fellowship may be supported by new forms of relational contact and new ways of interacting. For help in understanding the essential qualities of *koinonia* in this and following chapters, we're going to turn to the theological work of Jürgen Moltmann, which grounds *koinonia* in the Trinity, rather than starting with historical human expressions of fellowship.

While teenagers seek full-time intimate community under the demands of networked individualism, in Moltmann's understanding, the church is called to be full-time intimate communion in reflection of the Trinity. Moltmann's ecclesiology—his theological conception of the church—is grounded in the belief that the church is not merely a social club that worships the Trinity, but the church is in fact intended to both reflect and be constituted within the communion of the Trinitarian persons. Human fellowship is both an earthly reflection and earthly manifestation of divine sociality.[11] So, to speak about *koinonia*, we first have to speak about the Trinity.

## PERICHORESIS MEANS PRESENCE

The inner relationships of the Trinitarian persons are described by the ancient doctrine of *perichoresis*.[12] Some theologians have described *perichoresis* as a dance; others use the word *interpenetration*, but Moltmann often speaks of the perichoresis of the divine persons as a mutual indwelling or a perfect presence. To indwell means to be fully present, and it is this definition of *perichoresis* that best communicates the ongoing mutual intimacy of the divine persons with one another, for one another, and within one another.[13] Moltmann sees the doctrine of perichoresis arising rather naturally from John 17:21-23:[14]

> I pray they will be one, Father, just as you are in me and I am in you. I pray that they also will be in us, so that the world will believe that you sent me. I've given them the glory that you gave me so that they can be one just as we are one. I'm in them and you are in me so that they will be made perfectly one. Then the world will know that you sent me and that you have loved them just as you loved me.

In contrast to a faceless or partial relationality, the Father, Son, and Holy Spirit "share themselves fully with one another" without limitation or restrictions, the selfless love of each person for the others thus permeating the others perfectly and continually.[15] Perichoresis is not static, but describes the dynamic nature of the eternal "exchange of energies" mutually among the divine persons.[16] "Through their mutual indwelling the divine persons are giving each other themselves and the divine life in selfless love," writes Moltmann.[17] Perichoresis, then, describes the full presence of the divine persons within one another through pouring out the self into the others, as each opens the self up to receive the energies of the others.

## PRESENCE AND COMMUNION

If the very nature of God is presence, it should not be surprising that teenagers created in the image of God seek relationships of presence. What teenagers long for and seek through social media is the kind of presence in which they can pour themselves out into others who will receive them, even as those others pour themselves out into them.[18] Daisy, too, longed for such relationships of presence, but early on in life she discovered that instead of receiving love and care from others she received insults, jeers, and taunts. Her response was to recoil and to maintain a posture of self-protection and self-interest, hiding her face from others even as she lashed out at them. Daisy is not alone. Teenagers long for full-time intimate community and relationships of presence, but have learned in a harsh world to protect and watch out for themselves. As such, meaningful ministry with youth like Daisy will not begin with the church's adoption of technology, but by living into our calling to be a community of the face—*koinonia* in reflection of the Trinity—and inviting teenagers like Daisy into our midst.

What might the experience of human *koinonia* look like if we make Trinitarian perichoresis our departure point? In other words, how might we describe in an ideal fashion the kind of community that teenagers like Daisy should experience?

When we look at the Trinity, we see that communion in its fullness is a matter of constant, free, and unrestricted sharing of the self in love. Communion is constituted by a special kind of interaction; it is the unrestricted exchange of energies, the self-giving love of all one has and is—and it is expressed in action toward the other. Thus, members of communion can be described as being in mutual embrace and fully present with, for, and within one another even as they stand open to the world.[19]

Far from merely belonging together (that's a club) or sharing a common purpose (that's a union), in communion, others share of themselves deeply, even as we share deeply of ourselves with them. In communion, we share the feelings of others with intensity, such that "if one part suffers, all the parts suffer" (1 Corinthians 12:26). Members of communion are bonded with the deepest of attachments, feeling quite literally a oneness of heart and mind and thought and action. The shared love for one another in communion issues into severe devotion, affection, and a radical commitment to the good of the other. Members of a fellowship, those who have communion with one another, seek the good of the other through acts of self-giving.[20] As a result, members of communion can be said to belong *to* one another, not merely *with* one another.

But communion goes even further than belonging to one another. It is not a matter of merely knowing one another—that's a connection. It's not even a matter of sharing the same will—that's consensus. Instead, communion is a matter of being with, for, and *within* one another. Jesus prayed: "Father, just as you are in me and I am in you. I pray that they also will be in us," (John 17:21). Being *within* one another may make sense for divine beings, but it seems conceptually impossible for humans.

# HOW HUMANS CAN BE PRESENT "WITHIN" ONE ANOTHER

What can possibly be meant by being "within" one another? It seems that defining *communion* as being "within" one another makes no sense at all. How can we possibly dwell within youth like Daisy? How can Daisy dwell within us? We are accustomed to speaking of sharing space, as existing beside one another in a confined area, but it is disconcerting and difficult to imagine being present not only *with* one another but also *within* one another. This sounds like nonsensical speak—but only because we tend to think of presence as physical.

We want to think about presence "as if we are there," but we have already seen in earlier chapters that life in a digital age has exposed the difference between physical and social presence, so that even teenagers are aware that physical proximity alone does not constitute presence. If we hope to understand how we might be present *within* one another, we need to take a cue from teenagers and move beyond equating presence and existence together in the same physical space. A few years ago I instituted a rule with youth small groups: "Be here or be someplace else." It is a rule concerning presence, but it was initially meaningless to many parents who interpreted the rule physically and responded: "Of course my kid will physically be here or physically be someplace else. What other options are there?" The other option was to interpret the rule, as many teenagers did, as dealing with social presence. "Be *socially* present here or be someplace else" is a rule that makes sense to contemporary teenagers in a world of presence parsing technologies. They understand that I am asking them to be attentive, available, and interactive with one another.

Teenagers don't think of presence as something that's purely physical; neither do those working in the field of virtual reality. Those who are at the forefront of virtual reality make a clear distinction between *spatial* presence (the feeling of being there) and social presence (the feeling of being with).[21] Theorists in the field disagree about exactly what contributes to the experience of social presence, yet nearly all agree that without some kind of interaction with another—giving and receiving of attention, action, or energy—that social presence does not occur. In other words, social presence is not a concept of space but a concept of energy, and particularly the directing of our energies. This, of course, is also consistent with how Moltmann describes Trinitarian *perichoresis*—as a mutual exchange of energies.

It is through understanding presence as *directing* our energy that we are able to understand how humans can be *within* one another. When we direct our energies toward another, we call it *attention*. When we focus our energies, or give our energies over in attention to others, we are socially present. Our energy—in the form of concern, help, comfort, empathy, love, and so forth—are all directed not merely toward someone else, but *into* them. When you give someone your attention, the energy you are expending affects and changes that person. Your energy is not merely released into the world, but it is funneled into another, becoming part of that person.

Likewise, if we direct our energy into another, give her or him our attention, we can speak of giving out of one—or all—of the many sources and kinds of the energy we possess. An investor might "turn his attentions on" a company and direct his financial energy through investments. In the act of making love, to turn our attention means pouring our energies and efforts into bringing the other person pleasure. To give our attention to our children means not merely to hear them but to listen with the intention of understanding what they are experiencing in their lives.

Attentiveness is the foundation of being present *within* one another, though not yet the fullness of it. When we direct all of our energy in various forms—care, material resources, emotional resources—into another, then we have a level of presence with and for them. The fullness of presence, being *within* another happens when we also direct our love toward them.[22] "Those who love are not in themselves but in others; those who are loved give others free space to live in them," writes Moltmann.[23] This is the human approximation of the perichoretic presence of the Trinitarian persons *within* one another. Presence is not produced simply by sitting together in the same space. Rather, to be present with and within someone means actively giving of oneself for the other.

## BEING WITHIN ONE ANOTHER

Moltmann points to Pentecost and the communion born of the Spirit as an earthly example of presence conceived as *being within* one another. The community that lived together "of one heart and soul" (Acts 4:32, NRSV) and held everything in common is the "social expression of the new trinitarian experience of God."[24] The disciples' formation of the Acts 2 community overflowed naturally from their experience of the indwelling presence of the Holy Spirit. When we live in God, when the presence of God indwells us, we give up our fear of others, our self-protective ways, and our very possessions in order to give of ourselves to others, to invite them into presence and love with us—and with God.

Daisy came to experience the first thin strands of this through the efforts of Kari and Savannah. Somehow they came to recognize that Daisy was alone. "She didn't have any real friends, so we decided to be her friends," they would later report. Kari, Savannah, and Daisy were an unlikely trio. Kari was a cheerleader—pretty, thin, and very popular. Savannah was the captain of the volleyball team—athletic, smart, and a student council member. They both ran in the social circles Daisy most feared and therefore mercilessly criticized. But Kari and Savannah decided to brave the abuse Daisy dished out at them, along with the loss in social standing that socializing with her brought them. They directed their energy into Daisy by giving her their attention and love. They started walking the halls with her, eating lunch with her, and actually taking an interest in her life. Maybe most shocking for Daisy, they invited her to join them after school. She couldn't remember the last time she had been invited anywhere—much less by two girls who were so different from her. Daisy gradually lowered her defenses and began to allow herself to receive the love and care offered by two girls she was coming to accept as true friends. For the first time she began to experience a relationship that was more than faceless, one in which she felt known and loved. As Daisy began to experience the presence of Kari and Savannah in her life, she slowly revealed herself and the secrets hidden behind the tough façade she presented at school.

# EPICLETIC PRACTICES OF SELF-GIVING

As we have come to understand through the perichoresis of the divine persons, presence is not a passive activity, but involves pouring out one's energies into another even as we receive the energies of others poured into us. Presence is a matter of giving others our attention through listening, concern, comfort, empathy, help, and ultimately love. Epicletic practices of self-giving are those that encourage teens to care for others as individuals in real and tangible ways. Such practices will prod youth to bear the burdens of others (Galatians 6) and "be happy with those who are happy, and cry with those who are crying" (Romans 12:15). In a networked world, knowledge of someone's situation is vastly different from being present to give physical help and social support. It is one thing to like a post on Facebook and quite another to carry one another's burdens while physically walking alongside through the trials of life. Congregations that commit mutually together to practices of sharing in the trials and burdens of one another engage simultaneously in epiclesis that calls upon the Holy Spirit to transform the community into communion together.

To be involved in relational youth ministry in an age of networked individualism means more than youth leaders being vaguely relational with teenagers. It involves *encouraging youth to be fully relational with one another* by sponsoring practices that help involve them in one another's lives and the lives of other congregants as well. Many youth ministries have encouraged teenagers to help others through mission work or to find a place of service in the structured ministries of the church. We should also encourage youth to help one another as individuals and to pour out their gifts and abilities for their peers and for other members of the church as individuals. It's one thing to determine a teenager's spiritual gifts or abilities and try to match them with some form of ministry structure within the church. It's quite another thing to call on youth to carry one another's burdens and to be involved in knowing and caring for individuals in real ways. Practices that encourage youth to be involved in one another's lives and to care for others as individuals are practices that move them toward relationships of presence rather than partial connection.

When Kari and Savannah learned one afternoon that Daisy spent nearly every afternoon and evening babysitting for her absent mom and deadbeat stepfather, they asked if they could help. They began going to Daisy's house to help her wrangle her little brothers while her parents were absent. They were unable to change Daisy's circumstances—she was babysitting nearly 25 hours a week—but they were able to enter her situation and give their attention and presence. It wasn't enough for Kari and Savannah to listen to Daisy's plight or to empathize with her; but by directing their energy and attention to Daisy, they became present with her. They didn't need to consult their spiritual gifts or to interface with an established ministry of the church. They simply involved themselves in Daisy's disrupted world.

Epicletic practices of self-giving don't always have to be individual. Rather the whole community can engage in them together. Practices that move us toward the experience of not merely being with another, but *within* one another, are the kinds of epicletic practices which will open us most fully to the Spirit's communion-making work in our midst. This means practices where teenagers not only listen to one another but also commit their energies to being present within the lives of others both corporately and individually.

When Robert shared one evening that he had decided to search for his dad, his small group fell silent and listened to his story. "All I know is that my mom met some guy on vacation when she was nineteen," he told them. "He was in the Navy, his name was Ted, and she lost contact with him before I was even born. I don't want anything from him. I just want to know where I came from, and I want him to know that I'm here."

It was significant for Robert's small group to listen to his story and to voice some prayers for him that evening. But what they did over the next few weeks let Robert know he was not alone. At the urging of their small group leader, the guys started to think of ways they could help Robert. A few of them began collecting money so Robert could pay an online investigation service. Another guy in the group had the idea of posting ads on Craigslist; it was a longshot, but it was the effort that counted. Yet another student said he had an uncle who was a private eye and that he'd get Robert in touch with him. For several weeks the guys' small group leader continued to lift up Robert's search in prayer and to urge the group members to find ways to tangibly give of themselves to help Robert in the search for his dad.

In the end, Robert found his dad, though it was ultimately his mom who tracked him down and not the efforts of the guys' small group. But that didn't matter. Practices in which teenagers give one another their full attention by listening to one another's words and hearts and manifesting their love and concern in tangible ways can serve as epiclesis, crying out to the Holy Spirit to make them communion together. Together these guys became present with, for, and within one another through acts of love that began with their care of Robert.

What does this signal for youth ministries? We don't necessarily need to craft an active social media presence. Instead, youth ministries need to become what David Ford calls communities of the face—places where teenagers are known and cared for, even as they are invited to pour their energies into the lives of others. Practices that call youth to self-giving on behalf of one another can dislodge youth from self-protective actions even as they function as a call for the Holy Spirit to transform students into a people who indwell one another. While we cannot create communion, we can position our youth and our churches to be drawn into communion by the presence and work of God.

1. For a discussion of studies showing that large networks can provide more social support, see *Networked*, by Rainie and Wellman, Chapter 10.
2. As Marshall McLuhan once observed, "North Americans go out to be private—in streets where no one greets one another—but they stay inside to be public—to meet their friends and relatives." See *http://hbanaszak.mjr.uw.edu.pl/TempTxt/Wellman_xxxx_An%20Introduction%20to%20Networks%20 in%20the%20Global%20Villa.htm*. As such, American culture can be characterized as a faceless, face-to-face society, a society in which we interact with others, but in such impersonal ways that they might as well not have faces at all. Additionally, under the person-to-person community of networked individualism, physical public space becomes even more relationally vacated because it is now not even merely somewhere we pass through, serendipitously encountering others, rather public physical space is actually used to make private connection. When we listen to music privately on headphones, conduct personal phone calls in public spaces, sit by oneself in a coffee shop texting—all these are examples of ways in which we use public space as a place to connect privately with those who are elsewhere.
3. *The Saturated Self: Dilemmas of Identity in Contemporary Life*, by Kenneth J. Gergen (Basic Books, 2000) provides a discussion of relational overload from technological culture resulting in partial relationships.
4. *Self and Salvation: Being Transformed*, by David Ford (Cambridge University Press, 1999); page 21.

5. Transcript of AOL Instant Message conversation with Melissa, September 2007; name changed to obscure identity.

6. See also, "Small Networks and High Isolation? A Reexamination of American Discussion Networks," by Matthew Brashears in *Social Networks*, Volume 33, Issue 4, October 2011; pages 331–341. Also see *http://www.cbsnews.com/news/the-lonely-states-of-america/*.

7. "Declining Loneliness Over Time: Evidence From American Colleges and High Schools," by Clark, D.M.T., Loxton, N.J., Tobin, S.J., in *Personality and Social Psychology Bulletin*, Vol 41. No 1, 2014; page 9.

8. *Self and Salvation*, Ford, page 23.

9. *Self and Salvation*, Ford, page 23. Ford borrows this phrase from Edward Farley.

10. *Pilgrimage of Love: Moltmann on the Trinity and Christian Life*, by Joy Ann McDougall (Oxford University Press, 2005); page 119. Moltmann does not posit that the relationships among the divine persons should be constituted in certain forms of human relationship. So, for example, Moltmann ultimately rejects the notion that the nuclear family (man, woman, child) best represent the imago Trinitatis, the image of the Trinity. Rather, he "predicates his analogy of fellowship in terms of the quality of relationships among the divine persons." The correspondence between divine and human persons is "a correspondence between the patterns of fellowship that constitute the inner divine life with those that can be actualized in the human community." Humans are not imago Trinitatis when assembled in particular relational configuration or structure, rather "human beings are imago trinitatis and only correspond to the triune God when they are united with one another." See *God in Creation*, by Jürgen Moltmann (Fortress Press, 1993); page 241. The external structure does not create imago Trinitatis, rather it is the nature of personal relationships as they exist among people.

11. *The Trinity and the Kingdom*, by Jürgen Moltmann (Fortress Press, 1993); page 8.

12. John of Damascus was the first theologian to employ *perichoresis* as a concept in relation to the Trinitarian persons.

13. Moltmann finds perichoresis properly balances God's threeness and unity in dialectic tension without reducing God to either three or one. It is important for us to realize that perichoresis does not just describe the relationality of the divine persons, but also their "intimate indwelling" of the persons in one another (see *The Trinity and the Kingdom*, by Moltmann, page 169). To reduce perichoresis to merely a concept by which we speak of the relationality of the divine persons is to miss the fullness of the doctrine. Moltmann points to Jesus' words in the Gospel of John to further elucidate this reality.

14. Alongside the Gospel of John, Moltmann credits his particular take on perichoresis as originating with John of Damascus.

15. *The Trinity and the Kingdom*, Moltmann, page 57. "The loving person enters entirely into the other whom he loves, but in that other he is entirely himself. The unselfishness of love lies in the loving person's communication of himself, not in his self-destruction."

16. *The Trinity and the Kingdom*, Moltmann, page 174.

17. "Perichoresis: An Old Magic Word for a New Trinitarian Theology," by Jürgen Moltmann, in *Trinity, Community and the Triune God: Contributions to Trinitarian Theology*, ed. by M. Douglas Meeks (Kingswood Books, 2000); page 115.

18. This kind of presence coheres with Erik Erikson's explanation of fidelity as the abiding presence of others who are willing to pour into them even as teenagers are allowed to pour out their energies, gifts, and attention. Kenda Dean's concept of the "deeply spiritual search for another who knows what it is like to be me," is also answered in the intimacy of full presence. Or consider the frenetic teenage activity of maintaining network ties by commenting and posting, and hoping that others will receive and "like" it; though it is disfigured and corrupted, it is rooted in the longing for full presence we've just explored as teenagers pour themselves out, hoping to receive back from others. Teenagers are longing for presence, and in the Trinity, we find a definition and paradigm of presence with, for, and within one another that is characterized by selfless love and self-emptying.

19. *History and the Triune God*, by Jürgen Moltmann (Hymns Ancient & Modern Ltd., 2012); page 132.

20. *What Is a Person? Rethinking Humanity, Social Life, and the Moral Good From the Person Up*, by Christian Smith (University of Chicago, 2011); page 68.

21. See *Presence: Teleoperators and Virtual Environments* (MIT Press), an academic journal for virtual reality theorists that routinely explores the nature of the experience of social presence and spatial presence.

22. We might inquire as to why Moltmann does not point to sexual intercourse as a metaphor or analogy for full presence. I would suggest that the nature of sexual intercourse gives us one model of "interpenetration" and presence, but this model fails if we consider merely the physical act alone. The complete transparency of one to another that happens in the intimacy of a relationship may be physically expressed in sexual intercourse, but the full presence of members of that relationship with one another is not constituted merely by the sex act. Sex is intended to be a physical expression of a spiritual and emotional oneness; divorcing physical enactment from emotional, spiritual, and mental presence and interpenetration is why one-night stands and empty sexual acts fail to fully enact the meaning of sex. So, merely pointing to sexual expression as an example of indwelling and full presence provides an interesting mental image, but fails to capture the fullness of how we can be present within one another.

23. "Perichoresis," Moltmann, in *Trinity, Community, and the Triune God*, page 122.

24. "Perichoresis," Moltmann, in *Trinity, Community, and the Triune God*, page 122.

*Note*: At the time of publication, all websites provided throughout this book were correct and operational.

Social interaction that is meaningful "faces" one another as we share our essence and experiences. The evidence of truly "facing" the other is care and love for the other that is expressed in action.

# WHOEVER LOSES HIS NETWORK:

## BEYOND FEAR AND ANXIETY
## IN NETWORKED INDIVIDUALISM

Teenagers live in fear of losing their network. The burden to build a network and the possibility of failing can give rise to self-protective action born of the fear that teens might find themselves abandoned, alone, and disconnected. Networked individuals "cannot depend on the goodwill or social control of a solidary community. Instead, they must actively search and manipulate their separate ties, one by one, to deal with their affairs."[1] As has been noted, a personal network only exists by the successful effort of the person who builds and maintains it. Building one's network and acquiring social resources "depends substantially on personal skill, individual motivation, and maintaining the right connections."[2] However, what happens if the person fails? While some have focused on the joys of a well-built network, others have observed that constructing an egocentric network sometimes results in bitter failure.[3] It is possible, says Howard Rheingold, to be enriched or to "be exploited and alienated" by one's attempts to use social media to build a personal network.[4] But if you are "doing favors and reciprocating signals to the network that you are worth doing favors for," then fears of being alone and abandoned are mitigated, writes Rheingold.[5]

True or not, this advice does not actually alleviate the anxiety of losing one's network, it merely prescribes an outlet for the anxiety through the frenetic activity of keeping in constant contact with members of one's network. "Feed the people who follow you" writes Rheingold.[6] "If you want help in the future, help somebody now. Pay it forward," suggests Wellman.[7]

For young people navigating the waters of extra-familial relationality for the first time, this survival-of-the-fittest approach to community can send them into a panic of frenetic activity. Creating a constant stream of online content—whether posts, pictures, or comments—becomes a primary way for many teenagers to maintain network members and acquire social support. While creating a "feed of life" can be undertaken in an attempt at intimacy (as we discussed in Chapter 3), it can also be undertaken out of a manic need to keep the network interested and engaged. Youth ages 12 to 17 lead the way as creators of content on the Internet, with nearly all of them sharing content in some form, whether pictures, videos, blog posts, tweets, or status updates.[8] According to Pew researchers, "Profile pictures are particularly critical, with some focus group participants participating in elaborate rituals to maximize the visibility in others' newsfeeds and hence the number of 'likes' of their profile picture."[9] The constant production of updates, photos, and messages keeps a teenager's face before his networked audience, and there is a pressure for this to occur repeatedly, consistently, and perpetually lest the audience turn its attention elsewhere.

There is an urgency, then, to stay fresh, interesting, and different, and this contributes to the anxiousness of young people in a networked society. "It's so competitive to get the most likes [on a Facebook picture]. It's like your social position," said one fifteen-year-old Pew research focus group participant.[10] Fail to please the audience and you might find yourself without an audience. Lose the audience and you have lost your network. Lose the network, and at some level you lose the community that affirms and creates your very identity.

Content creation is not the only strategy teenagers can use to keep their network audience engaged. Some teens become obsessed with quickly replying to messages received as a way to demonstrate their value to network members. At the same time, making a quick response reduces the teenager's anxiety that their friends might slip away. Fifteen-year-old Kara is one who has dropped friends who don't respond in a timely fashion to messages, saying, "When someone doesn't text me back, I feel stupid, and regret sending the text."[11] Consequently, when friends message her, she feels the pressure to respond immediately—within minutes—and "definitely within at least 30 minutes," she said. These time restrictions flow from the fear that if one does not constantly assert one's personal value to networked ties, then they'll slip away and find connection with others who respond quickly and are available when they come calling.

There's been considerable discussion about how some of this behavior flows from the Fear of Missing Out (FOMO)—the need to know what's happening and to be a part of it. In research with young people, psychologist Larry Rosen discovered that "three-fourths of teens and young adults check their devices every 15 minutes or less and if not allowed to do so get highly anxious."[12] In fact, he argues teenagers are developing compulsive anxiety disorders driven by their FOMO.[13] However, such behavior also flows from the Fear of Losing Out (FOLO)— the fear that ultimately one's friends and acquaintances will move on and desert them if the person is off the grid or unreachable. The fear of nothingness, of being forgotten, and having no one is paramount in the lives of adolescents who can sense in real ways that the total lack of relationship is total death.

All of this suggests that networked individualism functions on a sort of karmic "you will get what you give" kind of basis. As such, it is far different from the operating system of grace upon which the church as the body and *koinonia* of Christ is meant to operate.[14] God's grace functions by repeatedly and continually giving others what they do not deserve. In an economy of grace, finding a place in community is a grace received, not an accomplishment of the self. It turns out that it is one thing to be the author of your own network, and quite another to be a member of the body of Christ. If we hope to minister to youth in networked society, then they must be invited into a community that operates according to a different ethic—one that sets youth free from the self-focused anxiety that networked individualism creates.

## BANISHING THE FEAR OF ABANDONMENT

To understand how the communion offered by God contrasts the anxiety of networked individualism, we must return to the very nature of the Trinity. We discovered in the previous chapter that it's impossible to speak of communion adequately without speaking about the relationality of the divine persons.

Moltmann contends that the Trinity is fundamentally open, which means that the love of the divine persons is capable of seeking out, indwelling, and drawing others into the relationships of the divine life. In the experience of the Spirit, God comes to dwell in us.[15] As Jesus is understood as God with us *(Immanuel)*, so Moltmann understands the Holy Spirit as "God in us" (and in the world)—the Spirit of Jesus that is able to indwell humanity, even teenagers.[16] In the pouring out of the love of God into our hearts, the Holy Spirit is not merely applied to our lives, but "we experience the reciprocal perichoresis of God and ourselves."[17] We are thus transformed in this experience, not by the Spirit of Christ doing something *to* us (as happened in the Creation), but by dwelling *in* us. We are enfolded into the life of God, and God becomes enfolded into ours: "God participates in our transitory life, and we participate in the eternal life of God."[18] Such an experience can be described as *presence* or *communion*.

Though at first pass such an assertion might seem wild, it is perfectly consistent with what we learned earlier concerning Paul's statements about Christian *koinonia*: Christians share in the very "life-principle" and living existence of Christ; his life becomes our life, and our existence becomes entwined with his.[19] Moltmann is merely helping us see the implications of Paul's statement in Trinitarian perspective. We are, through the Spirit of Christ, accepted into the "cycle of divine relationships and the mutual indwellings of the Father, the Son, and the Spirit." Far from building our own network of belonging, the overflowing loving presence of God incorporates us into the perichoretic network of God.[20]

Consequently, youth are graced with an experience of communal presence; it is not an accomplishment they must seek, rather the Spirit of Christ incorporates them into the eternal fellowship of divine persons. The overwhelming love of God, poured out in the presence of the Spirit, assures teenagers that they are not alone and that they have a place and a security in God. In this, they find an experience of community that doesn't arise from a network built by their own efforts. Through the Spirit they are incorporated into a community that is not fleeting and will not be dissolved—and teenagers do not have to fear that they will be discarded, or that their network community will be lost. As such, in the Spirit, the process of being released from the anxious self-concern for accomplishing the networked self begins.

"That sounds lofty," a parent of a teenager recently told me after listening to this explanation. "But I don't see many people—much less teenagers— being released from their anxiety by having some kind of lovey-dovey, mystical experience with the Holy Spirit." Good point. But I'm not suggesting (and neither is Moltmann) that teenagers need some solitary or purely spiritual experience of the Spirit that suddenly releases them from the fear and anxiety produced by networked individualism. Rather, it is quite likely that teenagers will first experience the persistent and unstoppable love and presence of God through the concrete actions and presence of the church as the communion of Christ. The church participates in the divine life as we are enfolded into the communion of Father, Son, and Holy Spirit. Thus, young people may come to experience the penetrating presence of the Spirit of love through the people who are communion together in the Spirit—namely, the church living as *koinonia*.[21]

This is what Kari and Savannah experienced through their church in southern Idaho in the years leading up to their encounter with Daisy.

They both had been surrounded and graced by people who loved and cared for them without regard for their status or accomplishments. Their place in this community was not secured by their individual efforts. Neither was it sustained by their ability to keep the members of this church interested in them. In contrast to attracting a network audience, their experience of community did not depend "substantially on personal skill, individual motivation" or anything they did.[22] Neither did their experience of community depend on "doing favors and reciprocating signals to the network that [they were] worth doing favors for."[23] It wasn't through their regular attendance, their contributions, or anything else that Kari and Savannah experienced the embrace and love of God through this congregation. It wasn't even through family affiliation: Kari had grown up in the church but Savannah had only attended for a few years on her own without her parents. That didn't stop her from being loved in the youth ministry, and by church members of all ages. The church they attended was intentional about making sure that people of all ages were known and incorporated in the life of the church. The youth minister, along with the rest of the pastoral staff, had worked diligently to create a culture in which teenagers were welcomed and loved by all. The effort to see all congregants as sharers in Christ Jesus had caught on to the degree that it was not uncommon for older congregants to approach teenagers and to adopt them as their own.

As a result, Kari and Savannah were released from the fear of being alone and the anxiety of keeping the community interested in them. They experienced belonging in a community that had not been assembled by their efforts; neither would it be dissolved by their failures. They had little anxiety or fear that there was anything they could do to lose their community because they had done nothing to gain its love in the first place. This opened Kari and Savannah to do something radical for Daisy.

## RELEASING OUR ENERGIES

When we experience the Spirit's loving presence, the result is a rehabilitation that opens us to God and others and makes it possible for us to be fully present with and for others in love. "We love because he first loved us" (1 John 4:19).[24] Through the love and presence of God, "unfree, closed, introverted people are opened" to live in communion together.[25]

In the presence of the Spirit, we are enabled to release our energies from self-preservation, privilege, and personal advancement—all activities born of fear and anxiety—and it is possible to expend these energies on others.

The experience of being incorporated into the life of God and the communion of Christ releases us from anxiety and fear. It is also the Holy Spirit at work in communion that replaces our self-protective impulses with love.[26] In communion, the anxiety and fear born out of a need for self-protection are replaced by trust and by an embrace of others. In the experience of communion, we find the freedom to entrust the self as a gift to others and to be fully present with them.

This freedom is both a "freedom *from*" and a "freedom *for*."[27] First, it is freedom from anxious achievement of oneself, freedom from compulsion to pursue one's own interests and needs. Second, it's a freedom for the other; a freedom to be truly present with the other without concern for one's self-achievement and security. One is free to give of oneself for another; truly free to both give and receive love. Being released from the need to accomplish the self, to gain validity and status, youth are thus free to truly be present with others. They are set free for relationality and for presence with and within others.

When Kari and Savannah experienced the unmerited love of God in tangible ways through their congregation, they were released from the anxiety and fear of building their own networked community. They also found themselves freed to love others. Previously, they had been fearful of loving students like Daisy because they feared being snubbed by the in-crowd. But as they grew deeper into the life of their congregation and experienced incredible love and acceptance, they were released from these anxieties. That doesn't mean they didn't lose friends when they started hanging out with Daisy—they did—but, they experienced that their personal value and identity arose from the communion of Christ, not from their network of school friends. The love of God and the radical belonging they experienced in their church prepared them and released them to take a bold stand alongside Daisy and pour their energy and attention into her.

## EPICLETIC PRACTICES OF SOCIAL EQUALITY

Determining what practices youth ministries and congregations might undertake to relieve the anxiety produced by networked individualism can be difficult. However, when teenagers who are convinced that their belonging is based upon performance encounter a community of social equality, they often are able to release their anxiety because they experience that their performance isn't the source of their belonging.

Practices of the church that subvert the common markers of difference (or perceived social usefulness and value), such as class, ethnicity, wealth, education, or age can become epicletic cries for the Spirit's communion-making power. Through such practices, the Spirit can convict us of our biases, challenge our conceptions of the capabilities of others, nourish our love for one another, transform our ways of being together, and call us to repentance for our acts of prejudice and subjugation.

In any human social grouping, it is a common activity (often subconscious) to designate "differences that signify" and to determine a pecking order, or to place a value on others based upon certain markers. In a community of social equality, people are not granted status and given love based upon markers of social significance. Rather, they are loved because they are sharers with Christ, and thus sharers, partners, members—one body—with us.

Christian communion is marked by radical equality not secured by one's usefulness or desirability, but by the interpenetrating, self-giving love of Christ in whom all share equally. Communion is a matter of being part of the body of Christ; we are affirmed as indispensable—but this is a kind of indispensability to which we are unaccustomed. We are indispensable because Christ has included us, because Christ's life and love embraces us, rather than being indispensable because of what we produce or the value that we add to others. This is an indispensability that banishes the fear and anxiety youth encounter in networked society.

In youth ministry we often establish markers by which we create a social hierarchy: attendance, Bible memory, service. Teenagers quickly learn they can earn our love and affection by checking these boxes and, in turn, these are often the students who receive the bulk of our attention. It's a natural impulse to give attention and status to those students who attend frequently, or whose presence makes our events great. We quite naturally gravitate to these students and shower them with unequal attention and opportunity because their presence boosts our attendance numbers and this makes us feel good. They effectively earn our attention by keeping themselves in front of us—something not too dissimilar to keeping themselves in front of their network audience. On the flipside, teens learn that after a few weeks of absence—and maybe receiving a postcard or two inviting them to return—we'll effectively drop them from our network. They'll be marked "inactive" or, in some ministries, even purged from the rolls.

Our continued love and care for young people, even when they haven't earned it through attendance or involvement is in itself an epicletic practice of social equality. It signals that the love of the Christian *koinonia* for them is not based upon their performance or fulfilling obligations, but is purely overflow of the love of Christ.

During my tenure as a youth director at a Presbyterian church in the suburbs of Philadelphia, there was one family, the DeJardins, whose three teenagers I could not convince to attend youth group or any youth functions. All three young people were painfully shy, and their parents were nervous about them attending youth events. Over the course of more than two years, I'm not sure they darkened the door of youth group more than once. After the fourth or fifth personal plea to attend, I stopped pestering them but continued to check on them. In past similar situations, I had just stopped giving time and attention to those whom I knew would never attend. But with the DeJardin kids, I decided to treat them as if they were the anchors of the youth ministry. If the family attended Sunday worship, I'd seek them out and greet them warmly. I'd write personal notes on the calendars we sent to their house. I attended the graduation of the oldest DeJardin daughter and snapped the family picture. Never once did they attend my youth ministry functions, but I didn't care. I treated them in the same fashion as the most committed youth in my ministry. Why? Because their place and value as brothers and sisters in Christ was not secured by their support for my activities, but by their status as sharers in Christ Jesus. When I left that church, among the stack of letters and cards I received was one from the DeJardins, describing how the love they experienced through the youth ministry had shaped the faith of their teenagers.

If we are to live as the *koinonia* of Christ, then we need to stop loving youth because of their leadership ability or the value they add to our small groups and events. We need to move beyond valuing youth based upon their musical abilities or their singing voices. We need to move beyond valuing youth because of their social standing at school or their ability to attract others teens to our ministries because they're part of the "cool crowd." There's certainly nothing wrong with recognizing the gifts and abilities of teenagers but, if we're totally honest, we quickly learn in youth ministry to shower the "useful" teenagers with special attention and care.

We need to become self-reflective about the way in which we value youth for their performance or contributions in youth ministry, choosing to bestow attention on teenagers who have done nothing to earn our praise. This can become an epicletic practice of social equality that actively works against the anxiety of networked individualism, even as it calls for the Holy Spirit to bind us together as a people who refuse to operate according to the social hierarchies of the world around us. We must actively combat the idea that young people will find a place in the church by attracting attention, doing the right thing, or being a "good kid." When we value teenagers based on these things, we fail to challenge the dominant social operating system, and we effectively tell teenagers that they must keep their network audience interested and engaged if they hope to be valued in our midst. The love of God, communicated through the body of Christ, is not earned through performance, but is graced on account of Christ.

The celebration of the Lord's Supper is intended to be an epicletic practice whereby we recognize our equality as we eat of one bread and cup and as we cry out to the Spirit to be transformed as the body of Christ. In speaking with college students about their experiences of the Lord's Supper, a common thread is the way in which the ritual can be experienced as, in the words of one student, the "Great Equalizer" that breaks down class, age, economic, and other social barriers. A college student from San Diego told me:

> *I think there are times that you go to church where [you] are just painfully aware that they're not people you would hang out with under any other circumstance, and I often feel that at the beginning of a service, or when I first get there, and I never really notice those feelings after. I think there's something really cool about the church, and then also the celebration of Eucharist, that is sort of the great equalizer.*[28]

Of course, as we learned in First Corinthians, not all celebrations of the Lord's Supper function this way, so it is important to be intentional in celebrating the meal in ways that proclaim the equality of those partaking. This can be one form of an epicletic practice of social equality.

Another way for congregations to engage in this type of epicletic practice is to emphasize the equality of ages and generations as the work of the Spirit. The fact that our youth ministries operate as separated spheres from the larger congregation (what is commonly referred to as the One-Eared Mickey Mouse), or that young people are often excluded from leadership positions, should concern us.[29] "A new equality of generations arises in this outpouring of the life-giving Spirit. No one is too young, no one is too old; they are all the same in the reception of the Spirit," writes Moltmann.[30] Practices that cry to the Holy Spirit in longing for an equality of ages might take numerous forms inside and outside the congregation. Many congregations could begin by repentantly changing policies that prevent young people from serving on boards and committees. In other contexts, the practice of intentionally including and honoring members of each generation in weekly worship services could function as such an epicletic practice. In other contexts, emphasizing the care of shut-ins and the elderly as a priority of the congregation could serve as an epicletic practice. Pairing teenagers (banned from many shopping malls without adult supervision) with a senior adult (who needs help to shop) could be a more visible way of uniting the diversity of the body in equality outside the walls of the church. "The Spirit-filled fellowship of old and young, men and women, and masters and servants is in its very existence a witness to the world"; indeed, it is a witness to youth in a networked world who through the communion of the church can experience belonging and community independent of usefulness, social status, or age.[31]

1. *Networks in the Global Village*, Wellman, page 26.

2. *Networked*, Rainie and Wellman, page 125.

3. *Networked*, Rainie and Wellman, Chapter 10.

4. *Net Smart*, Rheingold, page 211.

5. *Net Smart*, Rheingold, page 227.

6. *Net Smart*, Rheingold, page 229. The way we "feed" members of our network, says Rheingold, is "by sharing value when you find or create it, whether it is informational, social, or entertainment value."

7. Wellman as quoted in *Net Smart*, Rheingold, page 217.

8. The percentage of teens engaged in each form of these content creations varies greatly. For example, as few as 24 percent of teens may tweet, while 91 percent share photos. All of these activities, however, are considered forms of content creation and sharing. See *http://www.pewinternet.org/fact-sheets/teen-fact-sheet/*.

9. "Teens, Social Media and Privacy" (Pew Research Center, May 2013) at *http://www.pewinternet.org/2013/05/21/part-2-information-sharing-friending-and-privacy-settings-on-social-media/*. The Pew researchers described one ritual in this way: "As one focus group participant described it, when pictures are posted, at first individuals do not tag themselves. Only when some time has elapsed, and the picture has already accumulated some 'likes,' will a user tag themselves or friends. The new tagging causes the photo to once again show up in news feeds, with the renewed attention being another opportunity to gather more 'likes.'"

10. "Teens, Social Media and Privacy" at *http://www.pewinternet.org/2013/05/21/part-2-information-sharing-friending-and-privacy-settings-on-social-media/*.

11. Personal conversation via Facebook chat, June 28, 2013. Name changed to obscure identity.

12. "Driven to Distraction: Our Wired Generation," by Larry Rosen, in *The Free Lance-Star*, Fredericksburg, Virginia, 13 November 2012.

13. *iDisorder: Understanding Our Obsession With Technology and Overcoming Its Hold on Life*, by Larry D. Rosen (St. Martins Griffin, 2013).

14. "It's Not Who You Know, It's How You Know Them: Who Exchanges What With Whom?" by Plickert, Gabriele, Rochelle R. Cote, and Barry Wellman in *Social Networks* 29(3) (2007); pages 405-429. "The overwhelming direct cause of reciprocity is giving support in the first place."

15. *The Spirit of Life*, Moltmann, pages 195-196. "The Spirit of God dwells in you," (Romans 8:9, NRSV). In receiving the Spirit, we do not receive "a detached counterpart" that floats along with us, a conscience, a moral arbiter or spiritual guide; rather, in the experience of the Spirit, God is "all-embracing presence," says Moltmann. To explain this Moltmann appeals to Romans 5:5, which states that "God's love has been poured into our hearts through the Holy Spirit that has been given to us" (NRSV). This pouring out of love, says Moltmann, is in very actuality the indwelling of God: God is "'in us' and we ourselves are 'in God.'" On this point, McDougall criticizes Moltmann for failing to distinguish between the perichoresis of the divine persons and the perichoresis that happens between God and persons (see "A Room of One's Own: Trinitarian Perichoresis as Analogy for the God-Human Relationship," by Joy Ann McDougall, in *Wo ist Gott? Gottesräume—Lebensräume*, ed. Jürgen Moltmann and Carmen Rivuzumwami [Neukirchen-Vluyn: Neukirchener Verlag, 2002]; pages 133-141). McDougall criticizes Moltmann's conception of the Holy Spirit's interaction with humans as *perichoresis* noting that there is difficulty in using a term that speaks about mutually constituting one another to describe the relationship between creatures and the Creator. "Unless it is carefully qualified, the model of *perichoresis* belies this fundamental dependency that humans have upon their

Creator," writes McDougall. In short, it threatens to make humans mutually constitutive of God, thus threatening God's freedom and aseity. However, this can be corrected by recognizing Moltmann's use of *perichoresis* as analogical or metaphorical, not comprehensive.

16. *God in Creation*, by Jürgen Moltmann (Fortress Press, 1993); pages 101-103. Here Moltmann also distinguishes pantheism, panentheism, and his Trinitarian theology of the Spirit.

17. *The Spirit of Life*, Moltmann, page 195.

18. *The Spirit of Life*, Moltmann, page 196. This reciprocal indwelling is presupposed by Paul in 1 Corinthians 10, though there he discusses the intermingled life of God and humans shown forth by the reception of the bread of Christ. To help us grasp Moltmann's contention for divine-human *perichoresis* through the Spirit, the Lord's Supper acts as a helpful explanatory tool in this case: First, it is necessary to recognize that in eating the bread, we are not merely eating the body of Christ, but the very life of Christ. In reality, whenever we eat, something gives its life for us; the act of eating is always an intake of the life of another. When we eat of Christ, the self-giving life and love of Christ penetrates us, indwells us, and becomes present in us. We consume Christ's life and it becomes our own; Christ dwells within us. Or, might we say that we dwell within Christ? For when I eat and drink of the life of Christ, what is it that now provides me life? Indeed, it is Christ's life that courses through my veins and gives me life. Thus, in some ways it might be said that "it is no longer I who live, but it is Christ who lives in me" (Galatians 2:20, NRSV). "You are what you eat," goes the old adage. Thus, while we might say that Christ is in me (Christ has entered me, become part of me), it turns out that it is equally true that I have entered Christ by becoming one empowered by Christ, a self that is animated by Christ, one who dwells in Christ for "you have died, and your life is hidden with Christ in God" (Colossians 3:3). What Paul says in almost the same breath of Colossians 3:3-4 that "Christ is your life," and "your life is with Christ in God" corresponds to the mutual indwelling, and the reciprocal presence that Moltmann intends to describe in saying that "God participates in our transitory life, and we participate in the eternal life of God" (*The Spirit of Life*, Moltmann, page 196).

19. See 1 Corinthians 10:16-17.

20. "The Spirit does not merely bring about fellowship with himself. He himself issues from his fellowship with the Father and the Son, and the fellowship into which he enters with believers corresponds to his fellowship with the Father and the Son, and is therefore a *trinitarian fellowship*" (*The Spirit of Life*, Moltmann, page 237). It is worth noting that Moltmann understands sin as separation and salvation as coming to union with God, a "gracious acceptance of the creature into communion with God." Based upon 1 John 4:16, which says that those who abide in love abide in God, Moltmann understands salvation Christologically in terms of the Son accepting humans into his relationship with the Father and additionally as the Holy Spirit bringing people to participate in the love and life of the Father and the Son.

21. This is one reason why I've emphasized epicletic practices of the church throughout this entire book. Our practices can be oriented to call upon the presence and action of the Holy Spirit in order to communicate the love of God and draw young people into the life of the communion of Christ. To be clear, it is not the practices of the church that ultimately hold promise, but rather the presence of the Spirit communicated in and through the actions of the communion of people with whom the Spirit is present.

22. *Networked*, Rainie and Wellman, page 125.

23. *Networked*, Rainie and Wellman, page 227.

24. Moltmann takes as his starting point for the restoration of love the "human experience of *being loved*" (*The Spirit of Life*, Moltman, page 249); emphasis mine. "Does the active love of human beings not first of all acquire its power, its attraction and the space in which it moves from the experience of being loved?" asks Moltmann (*The Spirit of Life*, Moltmann, page 250). For Moltmann, reconciliation with God involves the penetrating presence of the Spirit of Love, thus freeing and restoring our ability to love God and other.

25. *The Trinity and the Kingdom*, Moltmann, page 199.

26. The Holy Spirit is a "vitalizing energy," and in receiving the indwelling, penetrating love of the Spirit of Life, we are enlivened (*The Spirit of Life*, Moltmann, page 195-196). The restoration is of the image of God in human beings. There are similarities here to John Wesley's understanding of the work of the Holy Spirit. Wesley understood the work of the Holy Spirit as enabling power for the "recovery of the image of God, a renewal of soul 'after his likeness.'" (Sermon 12: Witness of Our Own Spirit, by John Wesley at *http://wesley.nnu.edu/john-wesley/the-sermons-of-john-wesley-1872-edition/sermon-12-the-witness-of-our-own-spirit/*). Wesley spoke of God's Spirit truly and continually working on our inner selves, not in terms of mere moral influence, but in terms of empowering and transforming grace. This ongoing work is "God's breathing into the soul, and the soul's breathing back what it first receives from God . . . a continual action of God upon the soul, and a re-action of the soul upon God; an unceasing presence of God." (Sermon 19: The Great Privilege of Those That Are Born of God, by John Wesley at *http://wesley.nnu.edu/john-wesley/the-sermons-of-john-wesley-1872-edition/sermon-19-the-great-privilege-of-those-that-are-born-of-god/*).

27. The indwelling of the Spirit of Life is also the one who is "the freedom which allows everything to arrive at itself, in its own unique nature" (*The Spirit of Life*, Moltmann, page 220).

28. Andrew Zirschky, "The Eucharist and Young Adults Project: An Exploration of the Meaning of Communion Practices in the Faith Lives of Nazarene Young Adults Ages 17 to 26," unpublished manuscript.

29. "The One-Eared Mickey Mouse," by Stuart Cummings-Bond, *YouthWorker Journal* (Fall 1989); page 76. See also *www.ministrymatters.com/all/entry/2924/one-eard-mickey-mouse*.

30. "Perichoresis," Moltmann, page 120.

31. "Perichoresis," Moltmann, page 120.

*Note*: At the time of publication, all websites provided throughout this book were correct and operational.

# BEYOND THE HIDDEN SELF OF THE CURATED SOUL:

## FINDING FRIENDSHIP IN COMMUNION

"Snapchat is where we can really be ourselves," writes nineteen-year-old Andrew Watts in an article on teens and social apps. "There aren't likes you have to worry about or comments—it's all taken away . . .This is what makes it so addicting and liberating."[1]

Watts' viewpoint on Snapchat—the app that allows teens to send photos that disappear in ten seconds or less—is decidedly different from parent groups and the popular media who have labeled Snapchat a nefarious invention designed for sexting. One youth ministry pundit even remarked, "I've never seen a more dangerous application targeting teenagers."[2]

Despite research showing that most teens use the app to send goofy (and fully clothed) selfies, most adults can't fathom a legitimate use for

Snapchat because they can't fathom the social pressure of growing up in a networked world.[3] What use could self-destructing pictures possibly have? The adult mind immediately turns to sex, but teenagers think about freedom from net permanence and the harsh judgment that often comes with sharing digital photos. Set free from the burden of looking great, teenagers turn on Snapchat and take off—not their clothes—but their facades. On Snapchat, "It's the real you," writes Watts.

Where can teens fully be who they are? That's a question we should be able to answer by pointing to the church as *koinonia*, a people called to be fully present with one another. However, first we must understand the hidden selves of networked youth.

## BRANDED, CURATED, AND HIDDEN

Much has been said in popular culture about teenagers' intimate self-disclosure through social media, but less has been said about the way in which they practice strategic self-concealment.[4] To ensure the survival and flourishing of their network, youth are pushed toward self-presentations that are carefully crafted, smoothed, and buffed to project a particular persona.[5] "You need to pretend that you're something that you're not," said a fifteen-year-old female in a recent Pew study about online friending.[6] After all, if one presents a distasteful version of the self, then the audience might lose interest or leave. In another study conducted jointly by the Girls Scouts of America and Pew Research, 74 percent of girls said that "most girls my age use social networking sites to make themselves look cooler than they are." Sadly, the study also found that girls downplay both their intelligence and their efforts to be a good influence as ways to attract attention and appear "cooler" to their peers.[7]

In a networked world, teenagers must envision their desired place in the social order, and then "attempt to garner the reactions to their performances that match their vision."[8] Thus, impression management through selective concealment and disclosure is an important skill.[9] "A lot of people either glorify themselves on Facebook or post stuff that doesn't show what they're really about, or them in real life," remarked a sixteen-year-old boy in a recent study.[10] What he's talking about is personal branding, "the process by which individuals and entrepreneurs differentiate themselves and stand out from a crowd by identifying and articulating their unique value proposition."[11] Personal branding does not require logo-embossed apparel or business cards, but instead careful positioning to make the self appear unique, interesting, and valuable to both current and potential network members.

Closely related is the strategy of self-curation. While branding focuses on presenting the self as a unified whole, curation focuses on hiding aspects of the self not in line with the brand and that might repel others.[12] Curation can take the form of carefully selecting one's "likes" in music or movies, making sure you're tagged in only the most flattering posts and pictures, and immediately striking your best pose anytime a camera comes into view. If you don't look quite right in that "candid" photo, the need for curation makes it acceptable to demand retakes to get a picture both candid and flattering. In a networked world, appearing authentic requires hard work.[13]

Whether by branding or curating, social media assists teenagers in crafting the self fit for public consumption. "If I look good in a picture, I'll put it up," said a seventeen-year-old boy in a Pew study. But "[if a photo has less than 20 likes], take it down," said a fourteen-year-old girl.[14] More than half of online teens have decided to remove content due to concerns about their popularity and reputation.[15]

The self in networked culture is thus a production, a carefully staged persona—a mythic projection meant to convey a chosen identity.[16] However, this also means that youth are compelled to hide and suppress aspects of their true selves.[17] At first glance self-branding appears to be the way to tell the world that one is valuable, unique, and interesting—a real individual. Yet it actually requires hiding aspects of the real self in order to present an ideal self. Many teenagers experience this, and Daisy was no exception.

## DAISY'S HIDDEN SELF

Daisy had carefully managed her brand, positioning herself as the tough, sharp-tongued critic who wasn't afraid of eviscerating anyone who crossed her path. This attracted a certain kind of attention, as well as a certain kind of follower. At the same time, it gave her a buffer against the merciless teasing she'd experienced in middle school.

Daisy also curated and concealed much about her life outside of school. She didn't need to give anyone further reasons to mock her, so she kept the details of her life carefully hidden. After school each day, Daisy took the bus home to her other existence. She babysat her younger brothers, ages 2 and 6, on average 20 to 25 hours a week after school and into the evenings, while her mother and stepfather "worked" to try to make ends meet. In reality her mother was on and off disability, and Daisy was unsure of where she was or when she'd be home. Her stepfather, recently released from jail after serving time on drug charges, bounced from job to job, but spent most of his time bouncing from bar to bar. He too was rarely home—much to Daisy's relief.

With two absentee parents, proper meals were a rarity, and Daisy and her brothers struggled with severe weight issues because of the endless snack foods they consumed. Money was scarce, rent and utilities were rarely paid on time, and Daisy's family had moved more than a dozen times as a result of a string of evictions. In a southern Idaho town heavily populated by proper Mormon families with neat and tidy lives, Daisy's parents were considered pariahs. As a result, she did her best to hide her pedigree and circumstances from the people at school.

Curating the self is quite a bit different than being the self, and teenagers have a lingering fear that if they reveal their full and unfiltered selves, they will fail to attract an audience, fail to convene a network and, consequently, fail to be anybody at all. Thus, youth in an age of networked individualism are caught in a tension between longing to be truly known by fully revealing themselves and longing to experience community. They want to experience presence without hiding their rough edges and developing selves, free from the pressure to be "liked" or "favorited," and without concern for being bullied, judged, or demeaned. They long for acceptance and belonging, and yet teenagers pretend, hide, and withhold aspects of themselves for the sake of finding friendship and belonging. Apps such as Snapchat give young people a momentary glimpse of the freedom they long for, but it is an experience as fleeting as the pictures themselves.

If the church is going to respond adequately to the use of social media under the constraints of networked individualism, then we need to take account of how we can reintegrate the experience of fully being one's self at the same times that one experiences friendship in the embrace of community.

## THE TENSION: FINDING COMMUNITY OR BEING THE SELF

Networked individualism didn't create the tension between community and individuality; the tension between them is a long recognized issue in the history of social relationships stretching back to at least the ancient Greeks. However, social media gives networked individuals a heightened ability to resolve this tension through hiding the true self in order to gain friends and followers. Truly revealing the self might push network members away, so selectively revealing the self is the price paid to experience friendship. The question is: Can teenagers truly experience friendship when they can't fully be themselves with their friends?

Friendship, writes Moltmann following the insight of the great philosopher Immanuel Kant, always unites *affection* and *respect*.[18] Affection is quite simply the true "liking" of the other person: Friends are people who like you. The respect is for your freedom and individuality as a person: Friends are people who like you. Friendship, then, is always a free relationship between two people who like each other and who respect each other's individuality.[19]

This seems simple enough but, in fact, combining both aspects of friendship—affection and respect—turns out to be more difficult for most humans. Truly respecting someone who is radically different from you is difficult; truly liking such a person is even more difficult because "people who are different from us make us insecure."[20] It turns out that it's far easier to like and respect someone who is similar to you. As a result, human society is usually based upon friendship with people who are like us.[21] The principle of "like attracts like" seems to be so embedded in human society that the Greek philosopher Aristotle contended that it was impossible to truly be friends with someone distinctly different from the self.[22] While he assumed that unequal relationships could form between members of different social classes, ethnicities, and genders, true friendship can only happen when two people are fundamentally the same.

This limited or "closed" viewed of friendship still holds sway. While early observers of the Internet thought that the network might lead to a blossoming of diverse friendships, the opposite has been true. People tend to use the Internet generally, and social media specifically, to seek out friends who are just like them.[23] Teenagers may in fact get a lot of "likes" and respect for the curated selves they present, but that's significantly different from experiencing friendship that combines affection and respect for the selves they truly are.

# THE OPEN FRIENDSHIP OF KOINONIA

What is the antidote to friendships that require curating and hiding aspects of the self? In contrast to "closed" friendship, Moltmann observes that the New Testament concept is open friendship enabled and modeled by Christ who, though in "the form of God," (Philippians 2:6) was the "friend of tax collectors and sinners" (Luke 7:34). The wholly other God, incarnate in Christ, initiates a new form of friendship—true friendship between people who are diverse and unlike one another. Christ models and makes possible this friendship, which ultimately grants teenagers the freedom to be themselves in relationship with others.[24]

In the life and ministry of Jesus, we see one who confers respect and human dignity on those he encounters. In Jesus' day, society labeled people and valued them for the function they performed (teacher of the law and tax collector), or the sins they committed (gluttons and drunkards), or for the diseases and infirmities they possessed (leper, paralytic, woman suffering from bleeding), or for their usefulness and stature (a rich young ruler, a poor beggar). Meanwhile, much to the chagrin of the religious leaders, Jesus ignores such designations. He eats with those who should not be eaten with. He speaks with those who should not be spoken to. While the rest of the world bestows dehumanizing labels, Jesus respects people as friends. Jesus' friendship is not based on status, rank, or righteousness. In fact, Jesus enters into "open and public friendship [with] the unrighteous and the despised."[25] In his divinity, he "offers the unlovable the friendship of God," and in his friendship he "shows them their true and real humanity."[26] The nature of Jesus' friendship demonstrated an alternative social operating system on which his friendship was based. When we experience Christ's affection and respect, what the world says we are (tax collectors, sinners, teenagers) is stripped away and what we are is truly revealed: friends of God.[27]

Jesus invites his disciples into friendship (John 15:13-15) and extends to us who are "different" and "other" the friendship of the wholly other God. "It is the experience of God's affection and respect in the friendship of Jesus which shapes the Christian concept of open friendship."[28] The fellowship (*koinonia*) into which Jesus brings people is a fellowship of friends.[29]

## THE FELLOWSHIP OF UNLIKE PEOPLE

In light of all this, our command as the community of Jesus is to "welcome each other, in the same way that Christ has welcomed you" (Romans 15:7). "Through Christian experience of God and the self in the friendship of Jesus, the barriers of the 'equality' principle break down," writes Moltmann. "The friendship of the 'Wholly Other' God which comes to meet us, makes open friendship with people who are 'other' not merely possible but also interesting, in a profoundly human sense."[30]

We cannot live in the friendship of Jesus if our friendship is limited to people just like us.[31] Rather, we live and spread the friendship of Jesus when we meet "the forsaken with affection and the despised with respect."[32] Our faithfulness to our friends is the evidence that the affection and respect of friendship are true and real: True friends are present in misfortune, sickness, and in the midst of bad publicity.[33] "No one has greater love than to give up one's life for one's friends" (John 15:13).

The *koinonia* of Christ will be recognized by its unity in the midst of radical diversity. Truly Christian fellowship consists of people considered by society to be dramatically different, but it is held together by Christ's justification and acceptance of each; through the Spirit of Jesus we can become friends with those who are unlike us.

## COMMUNION BEYOND THE HIDDEN SELF

The basic relational bond of our networked world is the connection, but the basic relational bond within communion is open friendship. There is no need in open friendship to conform the other person to the self. Friends accept one another as distinctly different from the self. Friendship is open to the being of the other. And the friend is open to us. In fact, we entrust ourselves to our friends, even as we come to experience and know ourselves more fully through friendship.[34] The most important aspect of truly Christian friendship, says Moltmann, is that it "frees people from the false pictures of themselves they build up out of their ego-mania or their self-dispersion."[35] Both the teenager who doesn't know who she is, and the one who narcissistically can't stop talking about himself, are equally captivated by false pictures of the self. Yet, in open friendship, devoid of the need to hide or pose to gain respect, teenagers can be respected as persons in their own uniqueness.[36]

The task given to students by networked individualism is to craft an identity that is palatable for consumption by others. By contrast, in Christian communion, identity is not achieved but received through consuming Christ, eating of the one bread. Acceptance in the body of Christ does not require suppression or hiding of the self, but in fact the church as *koinonia* is a community in which we are free to be fully present to one another.

One of the gifts of communion for youth in a networked world is being fully present with others and able to be themselves without hiding or fearing rejection.[37] Where youth find belonging (unity) secured amidst diversity, there they are able to experience true presence, fully being themselves together without hiding. The communion-making work of the Holy Spirit does not result in a group of homogeneous, like-minded people from similar social, ethnic, and economic backgrounds. Rather, "there is neither Jew nor Greek; there is neither slave nor free; nor is there male and female, for you are all one in Christ Jesus" (Galatians 3:28). The work of the Holy Spirit results in a communion of unlike people who do not have to give up their diversity for the sake of experiencing unity.

The hidden self of the curated soul prevents teenagers from experiencing presence. We cannot truly be present where aspects of the self must be hidden, and we are unable to be ourselves completely. Rather, the curated self functions as a mask at a costume ball—to hide youth, to prevent the fullness of what it means to be present. The experience of communion, on the other hand, restores presence by freeing us to be our true, full, and authentic selves.

Where networked individualism leads to hiding of the self through curation, the mutual love of open friendship experienced in communion frees the individual from fear of judgment, thus allowing her to expose her true self and come to know herself in the process.

In the giving and receiving of love in community, we come to realize the particularity of our persons through the Spirit. In communion I as "*the I*" am able to be with you as "*the you*" in relationship; put another way, I in the fullness of my individuality am able to be in relationship with you in the fullness of your individuality. Surely this is the very nature of the presence that teenagers seek in a world of absence in presence, and also by their technological attempts to manifest presence in absence through always-on connectivity. Youth are seeking—as we all are—the ongoing experience of truly being present with, in, and among the other. Yet, this is the promise of Christian communion, not networked individualism.

## EPICLETIC PRACTICES OF DIVERSE UNITY

The community of *koinonia* brought together by the Spirit will be recognized by the community's diversity in unity—a unity of diverse people who have Christ in common is a sign of the communion of the Holy Spirit. Friendship that is not secured by "alikeness" is the gift of the Holy Spirit.

If this sounds impossible, we should remember that epicletic practices are rooted in the impossible and depend upon the Holy Spirit. When we engage in practices that point toward the ways in which we wish to be transformed, then these practices can function as prayers of epiclesis. Thus, not only is the communion of the Holy Spirit marked by diversity, but also our striving toward such diversity can be an epicletic practice through which we invite the Holy Spirit to work.

The first time Daisy showed up to youth group everyone gawked. Kari and Savannah strode into the room in their designer clothes and perfect makeup. Between them was Daisy, with her stringy, unwashed hair falling over the shoulders of a faded and stained T-shirt. A distinct odor followed her. Kari and Savannah didn't care. They introduced her around the room and ensured that she was welcomed like a guest of honor. For the most part, other group members followed their lead. When someone made a comment about the "smell in the room," Kari pulled the person aside and said it was inappropriate. The rest of the group got the picture. Daisy did not suffer any further snide remarks, and she actually experienced genuine inclusion. Daisy returned the next Wednesday, and the Wednesday after that. Before long she was an active member of the youth ministry and began attending Sunday morning worship services, too. Though Daisy didn't look, act, or smell like most of the others in the church or the youth group, the practice of welcoming and including her functioned epicletically by pointing toward the kind of open friendship we want the Holy Spirit to stir up among us all.

We have a bad habit of adopting the social structure of youth culture as the general structure for youth ministry. The same friendship clusters and subcultures of the surrounding youth culture continue to exist as prominently—if not more prominently—in congregational youth ministries. Some youth ministry experts imply that it is unnatural or impossible for adolescents to move outside their cliques and clusters, and so they assume such clusters must persist in youth ministry.[38]

I think we must challenge such assumptions, for "the Spirit of God does not respect the social differences, but abolishes them."[39] We should not sell short the power of the Holy Spirit to transform people—even adolescents—into communion together in ways that contrast and defy societal order. Surely, the promise in Galatians 3:28 held out by the apostle Paul is not dead: "for we are all one in Christ Jesus." Thus, epicletic practices of diverse unity in youth ministry will be those in which we intentionally seek to stand against the social strata and separation present in networked culture as we pray, "Come Holy Spirit."

In some ministry contexts this could look like fostering acts of reconciliation between private school and public school youth who traditionally jockey for status in the youth ministry. Alternatively, it might be a matter of fostering friendship and love among members of competing schools or neighborhoods.

In other contexts, epicletic practices of diverse unity might involve acts of reconciliation, dialogue, or celebration between members of different cliques, communities, or races.

In other ministries it may be that epicletic practices of diverse unity involve incorporating youth who are impoverished, mentally delayed, cognitively diverse, physically challenged, refugees, LGBTQ, or members of other groups who are often hidden from view. In all cases, it looks like receiving those whom society has decided have little value or honor and clothing them with the honor of open friendship (1 Corinthians 12:23).

As time passed, Daisy didn't smell any different or look any different. Her hair was still greasy and her clothes were still dirty. There was nothing about the way she presented herself or her "unique value proposition" that made her attractive to her peers or the adults of this congregation, and yet, she knew she was valued by them. This was a profound experience and it changed her. When Daisy realized her place in the community wasn't dependent upon proving herself likeable, her well-honed defenses came down. Her critical stance and biting words were heard less often. She was able to be herself and not the scared girl hidden behind a wall of defenses. Maybe most importantly, it allowed her to stop hiding and to share herself and her story. She began to speak about the fear and struggles she faced at home. She told about her stepfather's drug habit and her mother's depression, and the way that affected her and her brothers. "Most of all I'm afraid something is going to happen to my mom or stepdad, and then I don't know what we're going to do," Daisy shared tearfully one evening.

Daisy's experience of being incorporated into a youth ministry and church that loved her despite her differences also had a profound impact on the rest of the community. Other students began opening up about their hidden lives and the fears and struggles they faced. It was as if Daisy had become a touchstone, and the youth reasoned, "If Daisy is loved as she is, then maybe they can love and accept me as I am, too." When the youth realized their inclusion was not based on being right, looking right, or asserting their usefulness, they began to let go of their hidden selves and began being themselves.

Epicletic practices of diverse unity point toward a community of open friendship that accepts and incorporates others regardless of their identity. These practices also signal to youth that in the communion of Christ they can stop hiding. In such a community they can be fully themselves and thus fully present.

1. "A Teenager's View on Social Media," by Andrew Watts, *Backchannel*, January 2, 2015. See *https:// medium.com/backchannel/a-teenagers-view-on-social-media-1df945c09ac6*.

2. "Why You Should Delete SnapChat," by Adam McLane, (sic). See *http://adammclane. com/2013/08/22/why-you-should-delete-snapchat/*.

3. A University of Washington study of Snapchat users found that the majority use the app to send "funny content," or innocuous selfies. Only 1.6 percent of users said they regularly use the app for sexting. See *http://college.usatoday.com/2014/07/19/what-are-you-snapping-about-new-study-shows-snapchat-users-aim-to-be-funny-not-sexy/*.

4. "Information Disclosure and Control on Facebook: Are They Two Sides of the Same Coin or Two Different Processes?" See *http://www.researchgate.net/publication/24144686_Information_Disclosure_ and_Control_on_Facebook_Are_They_Two_Sides_of_the_Same_Coin_or_Two_Different_Processes*.

5. "Teens, Social Media, and Privacy" (Pew Research Center, May 2013) at *http://www.pewinternet. org/2013/05/21/teens-social-media-and-privacy/*. Social networking sites such as Facebook differ from text messaging in that Facebook tends to increasingly be used for presentation of the self rather than for intimate private communication. Facebook private messages among teens are on the decrease while public interactions and pictures via Facebook are on the increase.

6. "Teens, Social Media, and Privacy" (Pew Research Center, May 2013) at *http://www.pewinternet. org/2013/05/21/part-2-information-sharing-friending-and-privacy-settings-on-social-media/*.

7. "Who's That Girl: Image and Social Media Survey" (Girl Scout Research Institute, November 2010) at *http://www.nsvrc.org/publications/whos-girl-image-and-social-media-survey*.

8. "Why Youth (Heart) Social Network Sites: The Role of Networked Publics in Teenage Social Life," by danah boyd. See *http://www.academia.edu/1869588/Why_youth_social_network_sites_The_role_ of_networked_publics_in_teenage_social_life*.

9. *Networked*, by Rainie and Wellman, page 125.

10. "Teens, Social Media, and Privacy" (Pew Research Center, May 2013) at *http://www.pewinternet. org/2013/05/21/part-2-information-sharing-friending-and-privacy-settings-on-social-media/*.

11. "The Real Definition of Personal Branding" in The Personal Branding Wiki. See *http:// personalbrandingwiki.pbworks.com/w/page/16005465/FrontPage*.

12. While curation is often cast in the positive sense of "choosing for display," the negative correlate is that some things are necessarily hidden or kept out of public view. That is the way that I've focused on curation here.

13. *Alone Together: Why We Expect More From Technology and Less From Each Other*, by Sherry Turkle (Basic Books, 2012); page 183. Additionally, Rainie and Wellman describe the hard work required: "For example, if an individual does not disclose her needs, talents, and achievements she will miss opportunities to gain help or advance. Or, if she discloses too much inappropriate material about her life she may likewise find herself denied opportunities. And if she does not monitor what is known or said about her online, she cannot know where her reputation falls short of reality or where it could be bolstered." (*Networked*, Rainie and Wellman, page 269).

14. "Teens, Social Media, and Privacy" (Pew Research Center, May 2013) at *http://www.pewinternet. org/2013/05/21/part-2-information-sharing-friending-and-privacy-settings-on-social-media/*.
15. "Teens, Social Media, and Privacy" (Pew Research Center, May 2013) at *http://www.pewinternet. org/2013/05/21/teens-social-media-and-privacy/*.
16. *Oxford New American Dictionary*, "curate" and "brand."
17. At first blush, this may seem to contrast with what was said earlier about teenagers using social media to reveal intimate details about the self; but in fact that enterprise, too, becomes controlled by the need for impression management so that teenagers usually disclose only flattering details that will gain them an audience.
18. *The Church in the Power of the Spirit: A Contribution to Messianic Ecclesiology*, by Jürgen Moltmann (Fortress Press, 1993); page 115.
19. *The Church in the Power of the Spirit*, Moltmann, pages 115-116.
20. *The Church in the Power of the Spirit*, Moltmann, page 178.
21. Sociologists refer to this as *homophily*.
22. *The Church in the Power of the Spirit*, Moltmann, page 178.
23. "Social Selection and Peer Influence in an Online Social Network," by Kevin Lewis, Marco Gonzalez, and Jason Kaufman, Proceedings of the National Academy of Sciences 109.1 (2012); pages 68-72. Examples of web-based services that allow people to avoid difference abound, and online social networks are particularly well-suited for such applications.
24. *The Spirit of Life*, Moltmann, page 257.
25. *The Church in the Power of the Spirit*, Moltmann, page 119.
26. *The Church in the Power of the Spirit*, Moltmann, page 117.
27. *The Spirit of Life*, Moltmann, page 277.
28. *The Spirit of Life*, Moltmann, page 258.
29. *The Church in the Power of the Spirit*, Moltmann, page 115.
30. *The Spirit of Life*, Moltmann, page 259.
31. *The Church in the Power of the Spirit*, Moltmann, page 121.
32. *The Church in the Power of the Spirit*, Moltmann, page 283.
33. *The Spirit of Life*, Moltmann, page 256.
34. *The Church in the Power of the Spirit*, Moltmann, page 115.
35. *The Spirit of Life*, Moltmann, page 256.
36. *The Church in the Power of the Spirit*, Moltmann, page 115.
37. *The Logic of the Spirit: Human Development in Theological Perspective*, by James Loder (Jossey-Bass Publishers, 1998); pages 265-266. See a discussion on the twin fears of absorption and annihilation, especially among adolescents.
38. "The Missional Approach to Youth Ministry," by Chap Clark, in *Four Views of Youth Ministry and the Church*, (ed.) Mark Senter (Zondervan Youth Specialties, 2001); see also *Youthwork and the Mission of God: Frameworks for Relational Outreach*, by Pete Ward. (Society for Promoting Christian Knowledge, 1997); page 12.
39. "Perichoresis," Moltmann, page 120.

*Note*: At the time of publication, all websites provided throughout this book were correct and operational.

Teenagers in an age of networked individualism are caught in a tension between longing to be truly known by fully revealing themselves and longing to experience community.

# FROM SELECTIVE SOCIALITY TO OPEN EMBRACE:

## PRACTICING CREATIVE LOVE FOR THE ABANDONED

"You've got to do something!" the girl's voice sobbed into the phone. "Don't let them take me." The voice was Daisy's. The police had allowed her to make a single phone call while they waited for children protective services to arrive at her home. So Daisy called her youth pastor. She'd only known him for a few months, but there was literally no one else she knew to call. He asked her to slow down and explain what was happening:

It was a crisp fall afternoon and Daisy rode the bus home as usual. She was surprised to see both her mother and stepfather's vehicles in the driveway, but was confused when she didn't find them inside the house. Instead, she found her two-year-old brother—alone. He was crying and crawling around the house with a sagging diaper. From the looks of things, he'd been alone a long time. Daisy cautiously looked around the house, trying to locate her parents, but fearful of what she'd find. When she finally checked the basement, she found both her parents unconscious, with meth and drug paraphernalia strewn around. "I was scared and didn't know what to do, so I called the police. They've arrested them, but now they're taking us away," Daisy sobbed into the phone. "They said they're going to put us in foster care, but we might not end up together. I don't know where we're going. Please help me!" Her youth pastor promised to be there as soon as he made one quick stop.

"Do you remember Daisy?" he asked hurriedly, throwing open the door to the senior pastor's office. "She's come to Sunday morning worship a few times over the past few months with Kari and Savannah." The startled pastor nodded affirmatively and then listened to the details of the situation. "I know she's not technically one of us," the youth pastor said, "and she's only—"

"She absolutely is ours and, even if she wasn't, she has no one else right now," the pastor interjected as he picked up the phone to dial. "You head over there to be with her. I don't know exactly what can be done, but I know who to call to find out."

## DROPPING FRIENDS

"Follow people *only* if paying attention to them increases your knowledge, or inspires or amuses you," Internet sage Howard Rheingold advises his readers.[1] In the networked world, the relationships worth pursuing are those that satisfy the self. In building a network, it is expedient to choose and spend time on friends who are useful for producing the social support or position desired. Ultimately, networked individualism encourages viewing others as objects to be collected (or discarded) based upon their perceived usefulness.

"It's horrible to say this, but like if someone's not popular I'm probably not going to talk to them as much," reported sixteen-year-old Samantha from Columbia, Tennessee. "If they're, you know, unpopular, I don't want to be unpopular with them. I'd probably text them, but I wouldn't want to put up pictures with them."[2] While Samantha surely is not the only teenager who has ever dropped a friend due to lack of popularity, her approach is both easier in an age of networked individualism and more pervasive. Seventy-four percent of teens have deleted people from their social networks, and the practice of network pruning rises to 82 percent when considering teen girls.[3]

"Successful participation is not simply about having an account on a social network site but about having one with status." The alternative is to be alienated from their peers.[4] As stated earlier, such pressures leave teenagers anxious as they try to measure up and prove themselves useful, interesting, and "worth spending attention on regularly."[5]

If the church is going to respond adequately to social media and the rise of networked individualism, then we must rescue young people from relationships in which their value is based upon their social status and usefulness. The church's intended "social operating system" of communion calls us to defy this kind of selective sociality.

The first call Daisy's pastor made was to the police, and the second was to someone at child protective services. Within a few minutes he had his answer: "If we can find church members who are licensed foster parents, then the authorities are willing to place Daisy and her brothers with them temporarily. But I don't know who that would be." The entire church staff began making calls, putting their afternoon on hold, looking for anyone in the congregation that was licensed. They finally located one family and, by the early evening, Daisy and her brothers were on their way to the home of the Nelsons.

Although it was meant to be a short-term arrangement, it turned into something more. Facing serious child endangerment, abuse, and drug charges for using meth in the presence of children, it became clear that Daisy's parents wouldn't be regaining custody anytime soon. What was supposed to be a few days in foster care became months as the entire church rallied around Daisy and her brothers.

## THE OPEN TRINITY AND KOINONIA

Communion counters the selective sociality of networked society by standing with a radical openness and invitation for all people, regardless of their perceived social value and often times in spite of their lack of social value. Thus, communion further stands in contrast to instrumentalized relationships.

Communion is not closed to others, and it is not marked by the ever-tightening embrace of isolated and closed-off members; rather, it is further distinguished from usual forms of connection and community by its desire to include, integrate, and bring in. Jesus' prayer in John 17:21, "that they also will be in us," demonstrates that the communion of the Trinity "must consequently be understood as a communicable unity and as an open, inviting unit, capable of integration."[6] The dynamic fellowship of the Trinity is not a closed community, but an open invitation, and therefore, any expression of human communion must possess a similar openness.[7]

It is the overflow of Trinitarian life and love in the Spirit that affords the possibility of the transformation of human persons and communities. "In the gift of grace the Holy Spirit streams forth from the shared communion of Father and Son, throwing open their life-giving fellowship to human beings. The Holy Spirit renews human beings, by drawing them into the Trinitarian communion and transfiguring them into an image of it with one another."[8] The communion of the Trinity is constituted by self-giving love, love for the other that seeks the beloved, and ushers forward to include us in this open embrace.[9]

The loving self-giving of the Trinity is not bound within the persons of the Trinity alone, but overflows in seeking others.[10] Such communion, by drawing others in and sending itself out, is the very essence of presence with one another. It is on the basis of the openness of the Trinity that we are able to speak of God "with us" and God's assumption of humanity in the Incarnation. Human expressions of communion will similarly be marked by this open, integrating impulse that stands in contrast to normal modes of relational openness to those who are useful or desirable for our purposes.

When we turn outward as a community, loving those who are other, inviting them to simply receive our love without expectation or accomplishment, then we most fully correspond to the pattern and image of the Trinity. In the same moment that our energies are united in loving others beyond the communion, we find that our unity is emboldened and we come to love one another more fully. All this is from God, for we love because God first loved us.

The truly open nature of Christian communion distinguishes it from most standard definitions of communion. For example, in his book, *What Is a Person?*, sociologist Christian Smith defines *communion* sociologically as a shared existence characterized by intense "empathy, attachment, solidarity, devotion, affection and commitment to the other's well-being." The experience of communion, says Smith, advances "the personal fulfillment of those involved."[11] Much of that squares well with what we've said theologically throughout this book, but Smith only sees communion as an "interpersonal" capacity that engages one's personal social relationships, yet does not engage the larger world.[12] Smith conceives communion as a reality that only pertains to the closed society of the communion itself. The results of communion are not seen by Smith to overflow the bounds of the friendships of the communion.

In fact, this is a significant oversight, one that theology can helpfully correct, because as we have seen in looking at the Trinity, communion always turns outward in engagement. Communion that is contained by the ever-tightening embrace of its members is, as we learn from the Trinity, no communion at all. Just as communion arises between self and others by turning the self outward to the other (Chapter 7), so once it has arrived, the people who have become a communion together turn outward to the world. Communion is not merely concerned with the self, nor merely with the social relationships that constitute the communion, but in fact it turns outward toward both the larger social world of humans and the material world that we inhabit together.

Recall the story of Father Stephen and his Orthodox congregation searching for runaways on the streets of Atlantic City (Chapter 6). Their experience of *koinonia* together turned them outward with overflowing love for others beyond the boundaries of their church. Communion certainly advances the personal fulfillment of those involved as Smith contends. However, we must expand this to include the giving of personal selves as gifts of fellowship and love for all people, and "for the life of the world."[13] Communion that reflects and shares in the communion of the divine persons has results that extend outward beyond the members of the communion itself. It does not end in ever-tightening embrace, but in the openness of love.

## EPICLETIC PRACTICES OF CREATIVE LOVE FOR THE ABANDONED

Daisy's foster family, the Nelsons, announced that, with an impending out-of-state job transfer, they wouldn't be able to keep the kids much longer. "If the Nelsons are moving, then we'll get some other families in the church licensed," the senior pastor announced. Three families stepped forward, agreed to go through the lengthy process, and to take turns hosting the kids for as long as necessary.

Little did they know that months would turn into years. Daisy wouldn't leave foster care until she graduated from high school. Throughout high school she lived with families arranged by her church—a church to which she was first connected by Kari and Savannah and one that had loved and claimed her as a part of them.

While it might be tempting to think that fellowship should be characterized by an ever-tightening embrace (and internal focus), in reality the hallmark of Christian *koinonia* is turning outward in "creative love for the abandoned."[14] While networked individualism prods youth to seek a network of useful associates, Trinitarian communion is radically open to the other and seeks to draw others into the divine life—regardless of their perceived social value. However, this love is intent on actually incorporating others into the divine life, not merely serving them at a distance.

The community that is truly living as *koinonia* together does not turn inward to tend its life, but turns outward and becomes communion for the world through the Spirit.[15] The fellowship's expression must be turned outward, and just as individual members are called to express themselves and use their gifts on behalf of others, so the expression of the entire communion must be similarly turned outward. Its expression must ultimately move the fellowship beyond itself and toward the world lest it become ingrown and lose its true identity.

When the church embodies the ethic of the Triune God's radical openness, the church will find itself "at odds with a closed society."[16] The love of the Trinity is a love that draws and incorporates and is marked by radical inclusion of the lost and abandoned within the fellowship: It is one thing to serve the downtrodden and abandoned, it is quite another to adopt them as family and move into the neighborhood. Yet, this is precisely the friendship modeled by Jesus who quite literally took up residence in the neighborhood (see John 1:14 in *The Message*). The church of creative love for the abandoned is one of radical inclusion. "Charity" and service to others can merely be ways to hold others as less valuable or hold them at arm's length. Giving charity does not share self or life, but merely our resources.

On the other hand, the church turned outward in communion is not a church of charity, service, or random acts of kindness, but one that invites people into sharing their lives in communion, even as we give of our lives selflessly. The Incarnation of Christ reminds us that as Christ's body we are, like he, to enter into full presence with people who are "other," pouring ourselves out for them, inviting them to abide with us as we abide with them.

Consequently, epicletic practices of creative love for the abandoned are those in which we move beyond charity into including the needs of the abandoned in our own lives.[17] In many liturgies, the epiclesis in the Lord's Supper calls upon the Holy Spirit to transform and send us "into the world in the strength of [the] Spirit, to give ourselves for others."[18] As an epicletic practice we cry out in the Lord's Supper, not to give bread to the downtrodden of the world, but to *make us* the bread for the life of the world. And we are reminded that as we have been taken up into the divine life of Christ, so we are called to include others in this life.

Depending upon the context, such epicletic practices might bear similarity to the actions of St. Matthew's United Methodist Church in Memphis, Tennessee. This church, quite literally, incorporated a local homeless man named Guy into the life of the church. At the invitation of the congregation, Guy lives in the church building, eats his meals at the church, participates in nearly every church activity, and keeps an eye on the church building between regular meeting times and activities. When outside groups come to stay in St. Matthew's retreat facility, it is Guy who welcomes them.

In total, Daisy lived with four different church families, each one teaching her life skills she needed. At the Nelson's home, she learned personal hygiene—quite literally everything from brushing her teeth to washing her hair. At the Bennett's, she learned personal responsibility as they required her to keep her room clean, pickup after herself, and complete her homework. Her grades soared. At the Jordan's, she learned the value of and how to manage money. She saw firsthand how they ran the family business. They helped her get a part-time job, open a bank account, and begin to save for something she'd never considered before—college. As one of six kids in the house, the Stevens helped her learn what it meant to be part of the give-and-take of a family. And all along the way, she experienced what it meant to be enfolded into her church family as they supported her, prayed for her, checked on her, and raised money for her.

For youth in networked culture, the ultimate answer to their fears and anxieties is not the network they create, but a community that embraces and includes them as its own. As the church turns outward in epicletic practices to include the disenfranchised, teenagers are able to realize that they are not loved and valued because they are good enough, but because God's love is enough. In other words, when the church loves and incorporates the unlovable and socially discarded, by proxy the church frees young people from the fear and anxiety of trying to achieve value and lovability. Daisy's life was transformed by the embrace of a church that strived to be *koinonia* together by radically reaching out in unity and drawing in those beyond the boundaries of the church itself.

1. *Net Smart*, Rheingold, page 227.
2. Samantha in personal interview, August 2013; name changed to obscure identity.
3. "Teens, Social Media and Privacy" (Pew Research Center, May 2013) at *http://www.pewinternet. org/2013/05/21/teens-social-media-and-privacy/*.
4. "Friendship," boyd, in *Hanging Out*, Ito, page 111.
5. *Net Smart*, Rheingold, page 227.
6. *Trinity*, Moltmann, page 132, quoting the Gospel of John: "I pray they will be one, Father, just as you are in me and I am in you" (John 17:21).

7. *A Room*, McDougall, page 135.

8. *A Room*, McDougall, page 136.

9. Though beyond the scope of this book, within the scope of God's open invitation is all of creation; see *History and the Triune God*, Moltmann, pages 70-90.

10. Moltmann's understanding of the biblical witness of God is that God unites others with Godself, and as such, he finds it impossible to locate the unity of God in either substance or identical subject. Other concepts do not allow for the openness of the Trinity to which Moltmann sees Scripture bear witness. He makes recourse then to the concept of unitedness or "at-oneness" ("for only persons can be at one with another," *The Trinity and the Kingdom*, Moltmann, page 148).

11. *What Is a Person? Rethinking Humanity, Social Life and the Moral Good from the Person Up*, by Christian Smith (University of Chicago Press, 2010); pages 53, 68.

12. *What Is a Person?*, Smith, page 52.

13. *For the Life of the World: Sacraments and Orthodoxy*, by Alexander Schmemann (St. Vladimir's Seminary Press, 1973).

14. *The Crucified God: The Cross of Christ as the Foundation and Criticism of Christian Theology*, by Jürgen Moltmann (New York: Harper and Row, 1974); page 19.

15. *The Church in the Power of the Spirit*, Moltmann, page 194. In such a culture, the church is no less exempt from blatant self-focus. The modern church is self-absorbed, or as Moltmann names it, *societas incurvatus in se*—a community turned in upon itself. Churches are often ecclesiocentric in the sense that their survival, growth and internal workings dominate their concerns and they forget they exist for purposes beyond their own continuance. On this account, churches come to share these qualities with modern secular corporations, the pinnacle of closed societies or "societas incurvatus in se."

16. *Open Friendship in a Closed Society: Mission Mississippi and a Theology of Friendship*, by Peter Slade (Oxford University Press, 2009); page 22.

17. *The Spirit of Life*, Moltmann, page 235. Our communion "acquires its concrete form from the needs and distress of the world," says Moltmann. Because our fellowship is not merely a unity of members of the body of Christ, but flows outward toward others, the demonstration of our union together will look different in different locales. Communion, rather than suggesting a particular ecclesial structure or particular actions in the world, will always take its concrete shape as it carries on its calling in light of the particular distresses and issues of the surrounding world. When Paul wrote to the church at Corinth, they were failing to take account of the particular needs and distresses of the poor in their own midst and failing to care for the distresses of the larger society.

18. "Word and Table Service 1," in *The United Methodist Hymnal* (The United Methodist Publishing House, 1989); page 11. A similar formula is used in Presbyterian and Lutheran celebrations.

*Note*: At the time of publication, all websites provided throughout this book were correct and operational.

If the church is going to respond adequately to social media and the rise of networked individualism, then we must rescue young people from relationships in which their value is based upon their social status and usefulness.

# THE SPIRIT AND THE SCREEN:

## SOCIAL MEDIA AS A LOCATION FOR EPICLETIC PRACTICES

"So after all your research, what would you say is the key to experiencing community?" a friend asked over breakfast. "Get rid of these!" our colleague answered, picking up my smartphone and waving it. "Teenagers spend so much time on these, there's no time for anything else!" he chided. Of course, as I have argued in this book, technology is not the reason that teenagers fail to experience communion in the church. Rather, the blame lies with our blind adherence to a social operating system that operates contrary to the very essence of Christian *koinonia*. The apostle Paul did not shake a fist at the technology covering the table of the Corinthian church, as if the root of their problem were plates of bread, vats of wine, or the couches on which they reclined. Instead, he called attention to the ways in which their gatherings demonstrated a continued allegiance to the Roman Empire's ways of operating socially. Similarly, it makes little sense to shake our fists at Facebook, Instagram, or mobile telephones. These technologies do not determine the ways teenagers use them; rather their style of use betrays a continued allegiance to a social operating system that runs counter to *koinonia*.

Under the social operating system of the Roman Empire, bread and wine were used at banquets to delineate social status. But under the operating system of Christ, bread and wine were repurposed to become means of radical sharing. Similarly, contemporary technologies of social interaction can be repurposed as well and used to the ends of the operating system of Christian *koinonia* rather than networked individualism.

In youth ministry, we've attempted to use social media in a variety of ways:

- We have attempted to use social media to appear culturally relevant and attractive.
- We have attempted to use social media as means of mass communication to promote our events with youth.
- We have attempted to use social media as means of personal communication with individual youth.
- We have used social media to attempt to hold the attention of teens.

All of these come up short due to a single fatal flaw: We've employed all of them without first allowing our ecclesiology to determine the ends toward which social media should be employed. There is nothing distinctly Christian about any of the above approaches to social media other than Christian people using the media.

Instead of starting with social media, let's start with a church that is opening itself to the transforming and communion-making work of the Holy Spirit. Such a church can take a distinctly Christian approach to using social media by making social media the location of epicletic practices. Paul did not tell the Corinthians to stop their banquets, but he did say to make them the place where distinctly Christian ways of operating together held sway. Similarly, social media can be employed by congregations as the domain where epicletic practices are enacted.

For example, in America there has been widespread cultural condemnation of online and in-school bullying. Christians have jumped on the bandwagon, and I've heard plenty of youth pastors speak about the incompatibility of bullying and the Christian faith. I've heard others tell their teenagers to take a stand against bullying in their schools. Both approaches are good, but neither reflect on the calling of the church in conversation with bullying. What would happen if we started with the idea that a church, striving to be communion together, will engage in the epicletic practice of creative love for the bullied student? How would that assumption change our response to bullying? First, we recognize that it's not enough to speak against bullying; we also must creatively act in love on behalf of those who are being bullied. This might happen offline, but it is also possible to see social media as a location for enacting the epicletic practice of creatively expressing love for the bullied. This might look like using social media to express radical affirmation and love for those who are bullied. It might look like a group rallying around bullied teenagers online. The point is for social media to become the platform in which we enact the epicletic practice, just as we might consider youth group or a Sunday morning worship service as the context for epicletic practices.

On a crisp autumn afternoon in 2013, South Salem High School student Halsey Parkerson experienced the effects of social media used in ways consonant with the church's calling to creative love for the abandoned. While having lunch with Halsey at school the day prior, his aunt overheard a bully taunting Halsey, saying that he had no friends and nobody cared about him. That was enough for her to spring into action by posting a single Facebook message to a car club of which she is a member. The next afternoon, driving from places located as much as two hours away, cars of all vintages began to stream into the parking lot of South Salem High. School officials were initially alarmed as a traffic jam ensued in the school parking lot, and more than one hundred people joined in an impromptu car show and rally to celebrate Halsey. "It's just unbelievable," Halsey said while speaking to a television news crew that showed up to cover the commotion. "I now know whenever I get bullied I'll raise my head up and say, 'Sorry, I have too many friends to think I'm being bullied.' This is a glorious day."[1] If a car club can muster such an organized practice of love by using social media, I suggest the *koinonia* of Christ, in prayer and the power of the Holy Spirit, can do even better.

Social media could also be a site of epicletic practices of social equality, as youth and adults covenant together to express love and concern for those who have lesser social status or network value. Demonstrating love for those whom society considers of low status could happen through tagging them in comments and pictures, or simply taking time to send them messages of love and encouragement. Even these simple acts using social media can operate as epicletic practices by which we cry out to the Holy Spirit to be bound together in communion with others.

Epicletic practices of diversity in unity could be fostered by intentionally leading youth and adults into conversation together, or by pairing youth from various youth ministry subcultures to pray for one another on a daily basis using social media.

Guided by our understanding of *koinonia*, we could intentionally and continually use social media to affirm the value of those who find themselves devalued by networked culture. Social media is especially well-suited for epicletic practices of facing in which we engage with youth in ongoing dialogue as well as take the time for meaningful conversations and moving these conversations into offline space.

There are certainly other concrete ways to use social media as the site of epicletic practices. They do not need to be complex or earthshattering to be used by the Spirit. Each of the practices I've mentioned, if offered reflectively and intentionally with other members of the church, can be a way we cry out for the presence of the Holy Spirit and find ourselves convicted, nourished, and transformed as the *koinonia* of Christ. Online practices should not replace offline interactions, but they can enhance and extend the communion experienced together.

In a digital world, avoiding social media is as unlikely as it is unnecessary. Meanwhile, embracing social media as it has been used to promote networked individualism does not challenge the normal ways of socializing in American culture. If the church's response is outright adoption, then we fail to witness to the Spirit's communion-making power. However, there are ways to use social media that demonstrate our desire to be communion together, even as we cry out for the Holy Spirit to actually transform us.

## FORMING YOUTH WITH SOCIAL MEDIA

One of the most significant aspects of the Christian formation of young people is their understanding and practice of social relationships. In networked culture, Christian formation will involve exposing the ways in which the dominant social operation system runs counter to God's intended social logic for the church. By learning to use social media in ways consonant with the marks of Christian communion, teenagers are formed in the alternative social operating system of *koinonia*. Leading teenagers to use social media in ways congruent with the church's calling to be *koinonia* is an important aspect of Christian formation in a networked age.

Most Christian education pertaining to social media (if it happens) tends to focus on warning youth of the need for online safety and privacy, the immorality of sexting, and being generally nice online. However, those called to Christian formation have the opportunity to restructure the way that Christian teenagers (and all of us) engage one another through social media by helping them be transformed in their outlook and approach.

The goal is to see youth formed and transformed, not merely to temporarily modify their behavior. To this end, it has become commonplace to recommend media fasts to youth—periods of time in which they give up their digital ways and put away their devices. These times can be beneficial in helping teenagers to slow down, reflect, and as some have put it, detox from devices. But these practices don't do anything to realign youth to a different way of relating socially with others. Just as instituting portion control wouldn't have solved the problem with the Corinthians' celebration of the Lord's Supper, so instituting digital portion control doesn't get at the heart of the issue. The more pressing matter may not be figuring out how to get youth to put down their devices, but instead figuring out how to get them to use their devices in ways that are consistent with a Christian ethic of *koinonia* in which they "discern the body of Christ." Encouraging youth to use social media for different purposes will help them more robustly experience the alternative nature of the Christian community.

Attempts to form teenagers according to the nature of Christian *koinonia* while defying aspects of networked individualism could have significant impact. For example, challenging youth to question their motives behind self-aggrandizing social media posts or perfectly posed pictures could be a small way to transform their assumptions driven by the concerns of networked individualism. This could happen even as we encourage new ways of thinking about social media opportunities for acts of selfless self-giving.

Simply encouraging students to be aware of the negativity they portray through their social media use, or helping them pay attention to the kinds of people they spend time with online (and those they ignore), can bring awareness. Another possibility is encouraging students to determine ways to give of themselves to situations and issues that arise online, rather than resorting to trite comments. Hitting the like button is about as meaningful as the overused phrase, "I'll pray for you." Helping students determine how to go beyond the trite and trivial and to reach out to others in tangible ways is formative because it helps youth understand that *koinonia* is not passive but requires action.

Discussions of social media with youth shouldn't begin with the media, but instead with an exploration of what it means to be the *koinonia* of Christ and how that forms our relationships in all domains, whether those relationships are played out online or offline.

Each one of these examples, in subtle but important ways, challenges youth and adults to question the assumptions and effects of networked individualism and to choose to live according to an alternative order.

Many in youth ministry have misread the significance of social and mobile media, thinking that the church somehow establishes relevance to the lives of teenagers by appropriating technology for use in ministry. In reality, gratuitous inclusion of technology in youth ministry results from a misread of why teens are attracted to technology. We have seen that teenagers are hungry for continuous, meaningful relationships of presence that are not easily discovered in the disconnected landscape of networked individualism. Teenagers do not want technology; they want the presence and intimate community that social technology promises, and so they employ social media in a bid to achieve full-time intimate community and presence-in-absence. Unfortunately, their use of social media, dictated by the demands of networked individualism, leaves them anxious, separated, fearful of the loss of relationships, and ultimately deeply self-absorbed as they compete with others for relational bandwidth in the zero-sum game of egocentric network building.

In light of this, the church has to offer teenagers a form of community and relationship—*koinonia*, or communion—that contrasts sharply with the standard fare of modern society. In communion, youth are incorporated with others in the divine life of non-anxious belonging as they are released to give of themselves in love, while receiving the grace of God in community.

All of this gives us cause to be hopeful. Teenagers are seeking something beyond the screen, namely a depth of intimacy and relational presence with others. Far from being seduced away from meaningful relationships by the glow of the screen, the longing of teenagers for presence may in fact inspire us toward reclaiming the community of presence that God intended the church to be. If we pay attention to the longings of youth and heed the promptings of the Spirit, then teens may indeed find communion beyond connection and experience Christian fellowship beyond the screen.

1. The television news report of Halsey's car rally can be found at, "Facebook used to rally 100 to stand behind boy being bullied" KATU News, October 18, 2013 at *http://www.katu.com/news/local/ Facebook-used-to-rally-100-to-stand-behind-boy-being-bullied-228424401.html?tab=video&c=y.*

*Note*: At the time of publication, all websites provided throughout this book were correct and operational.

# BIBLIOGRAPHY

Alcock, Susan E. "Power Lunches in the Eastern Roman Empire" in *Michigan Quarterly Review*, XLII (4) (Fall 2003); 591-606.

Alison, Dale. *Constructing Jesus: Memory, Imagination, and History.* Grand Rapids: Baker Academic, 2010.

Anderson, E. Byron. "A Body in the Spirit for the World: Eucharist, Epiclesis and Ethics," *Worship*, Volume 85 (2011); 98-116.

Baron, Naomi S. *Always On: Language in an Online and Mobile World.* Oxford University Press, 2008.

Boase, Jeffrey and Barry Wellman, "Personal Relationships: On and Off the Internet" in *The Cambridge Handbook of Personal Relationships*, edited by Daniel Perlman and Anita L. Vangelisti. Cambridge: Cambridge University Press, 2006.

boyd, danah. *It's Complicated: The Social Lives of Networked Teens.* New Haven: Yale University Press, 2014.

boyd, danah. *Why Youth (Heart) Social Network Sites: The Role of Networked Publics in Teenage Social Life.* http://www.issuelab.org/permalink/resource/884.

Brashears, Matthew. "Small Networks and High Isolation? A Reexamination of American Discussion Networks," *Social Networks*, Volume 33, Issue 4, October 2011, pages 331–341.

Browning, Don. *Religious Thought and the Modern Psychologies.* Minneapolis: Fortress Press, 2004.

Byers, Andrew. *TheoMedia: The Media of God and the Digital Age.* Eugene, OR: Cascade Books, 2013.

Cacioppo, John and William Patrick. *Loneliness: Human Nature and the Need for Social Connection.* New York: W.W. Norton & Company, 2008.

Cacioppo, John, Stephanie Cacioppo, Gian C. Gonzaga, Elizabeth L. Ogburn, and Tyler J. VanderWeele. "Marital Satisfaction and Break-Ups Differ across on-Line and off-Line Meeting Venues." Proceedings of the National Academy of Sciences 110 (25) (2013); 10135–40.

Casey, B.J., Rebecca M. Jones, and Todd A. Hare, "The Adolescent Brain." Annals of the New York Academy of Sciences 1124 (1) (2008); 111–126.

Castells, Manuel. The Internet Galaxy: Reflections on the Internet, Business, and Society. New York: Oxford University Press, 2002.

Challies, Tim. The Next Story: Life and Faith After the Digital Explosion. Grand Rapids: Zondervan, 2011.

Chayko, Mary. Portable Communities: The Social Dynamics of Online and Mobile Connectedness. New York: SUNY Press, 2008.

Christofides, Emily, and Amy Muise, Serge Desmarais. "Information Disclosure and Control on Facebook: Are They Two Sides of the Same Coin or Two Different Processes?" CyberPsychology & Behavior. June 2009, 12 (3); 341-345.

Clark, Chap. "The Missional Approach to Youth Ministry" in Four Views of Youth Ministry and the Church, (ed.) Mark Senter. Grand Rapids, MI: Youth Specialties, 2001.

Clark, D.M.T., Loxton, N.J., Tobin, S.J., "Declining Loneliness Over Time: Evidence From American Colleges and High Schools," Personality and Social Psychology Bulletin, 41 (1), 2014.

Conner, Ben. Amplifying Our Witness: Giving Voice to Adolescents with Developmental Disabilities. Grand Rapids: W.B. Eerdmans Publishing, 2012.

Conzelmann, Hans. 1 Corinthians: A Commentary on the First Epistle to the Corinthians. Philadelphia: Fortress Press, 1975.

Coupland, Justine and Nikolas Coupland, "How Are You? Negotiating Phatic Communion," in Language in Society, June 1992, Volume 21, Number 2.

Coughlin, Sarah, "This is How Much Time We Spend Taking Selfies Each Week," *Refinery29*, April 24, 2015. Accessed at http://www.refinery29.com/2015/04/86241/women-selfies-average-statistics.

Crawford, Kate. "These Foolish Things: On Intimacy and Insignificance in Mobile Media," in *Mobile Technologies: From Telecommunications to Media*, edited by Gerard Goggin et al. New York: Routledge, 2009.

Crocker, Cornelia. *Reading 1 Corinthians in the Twenty-First Century*. New York: T & T Clark International, 2004.

Cummings-Bond, Stuart. "The One-Eared Mickey Mouse," *YouthWorker Journal* (Fall 1989); 76.

Dean, Kenda Creasy. *Practicing Passion: Youth and the Quest for a Passionate Church*. Grand Rapids: Eerdmans, 2004.

Drescher, Elizabeth. *Tweet if You Heart Jesus: Practicing Church in the Digital Reformation*. Harrisburg, PA: Morehouse Publishing, 2011.

Dyer, John. *From the Garden to the City: The Redeeming and Corrupting Power of Technology*. Grand Rapids, MI: Kregel Publications, 2011.

Erikson, Erik H. *Identity: Youth and Crisis*. New York: W.W. Norton & Company, 1968.

Estes, Douglas. *SimChurch: Being the Church in the Virtual World*. Grand Rapids: Zondervan, 2009.

Farley, Edward. *Good and Evil: Interpreting a Human Condition*. Minneapolis: Fortress Press, 1990.

Fitzmyer, Joseph A. *First Corinthians: A New Translation with Introduction and Commentary*. New Haven: Yale University Press, 2008.

Ford, David. *Self and Salvation: Being Transformed*. New York: Cambridge University Press, 1999.

Fuchs, L. F. "Koinonia: Text and Context for the Church," *Ecumenical Trends*, 22/Fall (1993); 1–15.

Garland, David E. *1 Corinthians*. Grand Rapids, MI: Baker Academic, 2003.

Geertz, Clifford. *The Interpretation of Cultures: Selected Essays*. New York: Basic Books, 1973.

Gergen, Kenneth. *The Saturated Self*. New York: Basic Books, 1991.

Girl Scout Research Institute, "Who's That Girl: Image and Social Media Survey," November 2010. Available at girlscouts.org.

Gould, Meredith. *The Social Media Gospel: Sharing the Good News in New Ways*. Collegeville. Minnesota: Liturgical Press, 2013.

Hart, Trevor, and James Torrance, Daniel Thimell. *Christ in Our Place*. Exeter: Paternoster Press, 1989.

Hipps, Shane. *Flickering Pixels: How Technology Shapes Your Faith*. Grand Rapids: Zondervan, 2009.

Hipps, Shane. *The Hidden Power of Electronic Culture*. El Cajon: Youth Specialties, 2006.

Ho, Shirley S. and Douglas M. Mcleod. "Social-Psychological Influences on Opinion Expression in Face-to-Face and Computer-Mediated Communication." *Communication Research*, 35 (2) (April 2008); 190-207.

Horsley, Richard. *1 Corinthians*. Nashville: Abingdon Press, 1995.

Horsley, Richard. *Paul and Empire: Religion and Power in Roman Imperial Society*. Harrisburg, PA: Trinity Press International, 1997.

Hütter, Reinhold. *Suffering Divine Things: Theology as Church Practice*. Grand Rapids: W.B. Eerdmans Publishing, 2000.

Ito, Mizuko and Daisuke Okabe, Misa Matsuda, *Personal, Portable, Pedestrian: Mobile Phones in Japanese Life*. Cambridge: MIT Press, 2005.

Ito, Mizuko. *Hanging Out, Messing Around and Geeking Out: Kids Living and Learning with New Media*. Cambridge, MA: MIT Press, 2010.

Jakobson, Roman. "Linguistics and Poetics," in *Style in Language*, edited by T.A. Sebeok. Cambridge: MIT Press, 1960; 350-377.

Jenkins, Henry, and Sam Ford, Joshua Green. *Spreadable Media: Creating Value and Meaning in a Networked Culture*. New York: New York University Press, 2013.

Jenkins, Henry. *Confronting the Challenges of Participatory Culture: Media Education for the 21st Century*. Cambridge, MA: The MIT Press, 2009.

Johnson, Luke Timothy. *Hebrews: A Commentary*. Louisville: Westminster John Knox Press, 2006.

Joinson, A.N. "Self-Disclosure in Computer-Mediated Communication: The Role of Self-Awareness and Visual Anonymity," Eur. J. Soc. *Psychol.*, 31 (2001); 177–192.

Kaiser Family Foundation, "Generation M2: Media in the Lives of 8- to 18-Year-Olds," January 2010.

Kearsley, Roy Church. *Community and Power*. Burlington, Vermont: Ashgate Publishing, 2013.

Keener, Craig. *1-2 Corinthians: The New Cambridge Bible Commentary*. Cambridge, UK: Cambridge University Press, 2005.

Kegan, Robert. *In Over Our Heads: The Mental Demands of Modern Life*. Cambridge, MA: Harvard University Press, 1994.

Kendall, Peggy. *Rewired: Youth Ministry in an Age of IM and MySpace*. Valley Forge, PA: Judson Press, 2007.

Kloppenborg, John, and Stephen Wilson (eds.), *Voluntary Associations in the Graeco-Roman World*. New York: Routledge, 1996.

Kreider, Larry and Floyd McClung. *Starting a House Church*. Ventura, CA: Regal Books, 2007.

Laver, John. "Linguistic Routines and Politeness in Greeting and Parting," in *Florian Coulmas, Conversational Routine*. New York: Mouton, 1981.

Lee, Michelle. *Paul, The Stoics and the Body of Christ.* Cambridge University Press, 2006.

Lewis, Kevin, Marco Gonzalez, and Jason Kaufman, "Social Selection and Peer Influence in an Online Social Network," Proceedings of the National Academy of Sciences 109.1 (2012); 68-72.

Loder, James. *The Knight's Move: The Relational Logic of the Spirit in Theology and Science.* Colorado Springs: Helmers and Howard, 1992.

Loder, James. *The Logic of the Spirit: Human Development in Theological Perspective.* San Francisco: Jossey-Bass Publishers, 1998.

Lounsbury, Kaitlin, and K. Mitchell, David Finkelhor, "The True Prevalence of 'Sexting,'" Crimes Against Children Research Center, University of New Hampshire, 2011.

Macmurray, John. *Persons in Relation.* London: Faber & Faber, 1961.

Macnamara, Jim. *The 21st Century Media (R)evolution: Emergent Communication Practices.* New York: Peter Lang, 2010.

Malinowski, Bronislaw. "The Problem of Meaning in Primitive Languages" in CK. Ogden & I.A. Richards, *The Meaning of Meaning.* New York: Harcourt Brace & Co., 1923; 296-336.

Marcia, James. "The Ego Identity Status Approach to Ego Identity" in *Ego Identity.* New York: Springer, 1993; 3-23.

McDougall, Joy Ann. "A Room of One's Own: Trinitarian Perichoresis as Analogy for the God-Human Relationship," in *Wo ist Gott? Gottesräume—Lebensräume,* ed. Jürgen Moltmann and Carmen Rivuzumwami. Neukirchen-Vluyn: Neukirchener Verlag, 2002; 133-141.

McDougall, Joy Ann. *Pilgrimage of Love: Moltmann on the Trinity and Christian Life.* New York: Oxford University Press, 2005.

McLane, Adam. "Why You Should Delete SnapChat," accessed at http://adammclane.com/2013/08/22/why-you-should-delete-snapchat/.

McPherson, Miller, and Lynn Smith-Lovin, Matthew Brashears. "Social Isolation in America," *American Sociological Review* 71 (2008); 353-375.

Miller, Vincent. "New Media, Networking and Phatic Culture" in *Convergence* 14(4) (November 2008); 387-400.

Moltmann, Jürgen. *The Church in the Power of the Spirit: A Contribution to Messianic Ecclesiology*. New York: Harper and Row, 1977.

Moltmann, Jürgen. *The Crucified God: The Cross of Christ as the Foundation and Criticism of Christian Theology*. New York: Harper and Row, 1974.

Moltmann, Jürgen. *God in Creation*. San Francisco: Harper & Row, 1985.

Moltmann, Jürgen. *History and the Triune God*. New York: Crossroad, 1992.

Moltmann, Jürgen. "Perichoresis: An Old Magic Word for a New Trinitarian Theology," in M. Douglas Meeks (ed.) *Trinity, Community and the Triune God: Contributions to Trinitarian Theology*. Nashville: Kingswood Books, 2000.

Moltmann, Jürgen. *The Spirit of Life: A Universal Affirmation*. Minneapolis: Fortress Press, 1992.

Moltmann, Jürgen. *The Trinity and the Kingdom*. San Francisco: Harper & Row, 1981.

Nakkula, M.J. and E. Toshalis. *Understanding Youth: Adolescent Development for Educators*. Cambridge: Harvard Education Press, 2006.

Newbigin, Lesslie. *Gospel in a Pluralist Society*. Grand Rapids: Wm. B. Eerdmans: 1989.

Orr, William and James Walther, *1 Corinthians*: Anchor Bible. Garden City, NY: Doubleday, 1976.

Osmer, Richard. *The Teaching Ministry of Congregations*. Louisville: Westminster John Knox Press, 2005.

Osmer, Richard. *Practical Theology: An Introduction*. Grand Rapids: Wm. B. Eerdmans Publishing Company, 2008.

Peterson, Eugene. *The Message*. Colorado Springs: NavPress, 2004.

Pew Research Center. "Teens, Smartphones & Texting," March 19, 2012.

Pew Research Center. "Social Media & Mobile Internet Use Among Teens and Young Adults," February 3, 2010.

Pew Research Center. "Teens 2012: Truth, Trends, and Myths about Teen Online Behavior," July 11, 2012.

Pew Research Center. "Teens and Mobile Phones," April 20, 2010.

Pew Research Center. "Teens, Social Media and Privacy," May 2013.

Pew Research Center. "Why Americans Use Social Media," November 2010.

Pew Research Center. Teens and Mobile Phones Survey, 2009.

Pew Research Center. "Teens, Technology and Friendships," 2015.

Plant, Sabine. *On the Mobile: The Effects of Mobile Telephones on Social and Individual Life*. Motorola, 2002, http://www.motorola.com/mot/documents/0,1028,333,00.pdf.

Plickert, Gabriele, and Rochelle R. Cote, Barry Wellman. "It's Not Who You Know, It's How You Know Them: Who Exchanges What With Whom?" in *Social Networks* 29 (3) (2007); 405-429.

Polyn, Sean M., and Vaidehi S. Natu, Jonathan D. Cohen, Kenneth A. Norman, "Category-Specific Cortical Activity Precedes Retrieval During Memory Search," *Science*, 310 (5756) (23 December 2005); 1963-1966.

Pope John Paul II, "The Family as a Community of Persons," in *Person and Community: Selected Essays*. New York: Peter Lang, 1993.

Przybylski, A.K., K. Murayama, C.R. DeHaan, and V. Gladwell. "Motivational, Emotional, and Behavioral Correlates of Fear of Missing Out." *Computers in Human Behavior*, 29 (2013); 1841-1848.

Rainie, Lee and Barry Wellman. *Networked: The New Social Operating System*. Cambridge: MIT Press, 2012.

Rheingold, Howard. *Net Smart: How To Thrive Online*. Cambridge: MIT Press, 2012.

Rice, Jesse. *The Church of Facebook: How the Hyperconnected Are Redefining Community*. Colorado Springs: David C. Cook, 2009.

Roesner, Franziska, Brian T. Gill, and Tadayoshi Kohno. "Sex, Lies, or Kittens? Investigating the Use of Snapchat's Self-destructing Messages." *Financial Cryptography and Data Security*. Springer Berlin Heidelberg, 2014; 64-76.

Rosen, Larry. "Driven to Distraction: Our Wired Generation," in *The Free Lance-Star*. Fredericksburg, Virginia, 13 November 2012.

Rosen, Larry. *iDisorder: Understanding Our Obsession With Technology and Overcoming Its Hold On Us*. New York: Palgrave Macmillan, 2012.

Schmemann, Alexander. *For the Life of the World: Sacraments and Orthodoxy*. Crestwood, NY: St. Vladimir's Seminary Press, 1973.

Senft, Gunter. "Phatic Communion" in *Culture and Language Use*, edited by Gunter Senft, Jan-Ola Ostman, and Jef Verschueren. Amsterdam: John Benjamins Publishing, 2009.

Slade, Peter. *Open Friendship in a Closed Society: Mission Mississippi and a Theology of Friendship*. New York: Oxford University Press, 2009.

Smith, Christian. *What Is a Person? Rethinking Humanity, Social Life and the Moral Good from the Person Up*. Chicago: University of Chicago Press, 2010.

Smith, Dennis. *From Symposium to Eucharist: The Banquet in the Early Christian World*. Minneapolis: Fortress Press, 2003.

Storey, John. *Cultural Theory and Popular Culture, 5th Edition*. New York: Pearson.

Theissen, Gerd. "Social Stratification in the Corinthian Community: A Contribution to the Sociology of Early Hellenistic Christianity" in *The Social Setting of Pauline Christianity*. Edinburgh: T&T Clark, 1982.

Thomas, Adam. *Digital Disciple: Real Christianity in a Virtual World*. Nashville: Abingdon Press, 2011.

Trepte, Sabine, and Leonard Reinecke, "The Reciprocal Effects of Social Network Site Use and the Disposition for Self-Disclosure: A Longitudinal Study," *Computers in Human Behavior* 29 (3) (May 2013); 1102–1112.

Turkle, Sherry. *Alone Together: Why We Expect More From Technology and Less from Each Other*. New York: Basic Books, 2011.

Van den Bulck, Jan. "Adolescent Use of Mobile Phones for Calling and for Sending Text Messages After Lights Out: Results from a Prospective Cohort Study with a One-Year Follow Up," *Sleep* 30(9) (September 1, 2007); 1220-1223.

Van Huyssteen, Wentzel. *Alone in the World?: Human Uniqueness in Science and Theology*. Grand Rapids: Wm. B Eerdmans, 2006.

Varnelis, Kazys. "The Meaning of Network Culture." *Eurozine*, January 14 (2010), http://www. eurozine. com/articles/2010-01-14-varnelisen.

Vetere, Frank and Steve Howard, et al. "Mediating Intimacy: Designing Technologies to Support Strong-Tie Relationships," First International Workshop on Social Implications of Ubiquitous Technology. ACM Conference on Human Factors in Computing Systems, CHI, 2005.

Vetere, Frank and Steve Howard, et al. "Phatic Technologies: Sustaining Sociability through Ubiquitous Computing," in First International Workshop on Social Implications of Ubiquitous Technology. ACM Conference on Human Factors in Computing Systems, CHI, 2005.

Visser, Margaret. *The Rituals of Dinner: The Origins, Evolution, Eccentricities, and Meaning of Table Manners*. New York: Grove Weidenfeld, 1991.

Wall, Robert W., N T. Wright, and J P. Sampley. *The New Interpreter's Bible: Volume X*. Nashville, TN: Abingdon, 2001.

Ward, Pete. *Youthwork and the Mission of God*. London: Society for Promoting Christian Knowledge, 1997.

Watkins, Craig. *The Young and the Digital*. Boston: Beacon Press, 2009.

Watts, Andrew. "A Teenager's View on Social Media," *Backchannel*, January 2, 2015. Accessed at https://medium.com/backchannel/a-teenagers-view-on-social-media-1df945c09ac6.

Wedderburn, A.J.M. "The Body of Christ and Related Concepts in 1 Corinthians" *SJT* 24.1, 1971; 76.

Wellman, Barry and Anabel Quan-Haase, Jeffrey Boase, Wenhong Chen, Keith Hampton, Isabel Díaz, Kakuko Miyata. "The Social Affordances of the Internet for Networked Individualism." *Journal of Computer-Mediated Communication 8* (3) (2003).

Wellman, Barry, and Jeffrey Boase, Wenhong Chen. "The Networked Nature of Community: Online and offline." *It & Society 1*(2002); 151-165.

Wellman, Barry. "Physical Place and Cyberplace: The Rise of Personalized Networking." *International Journal of Urban and Regional Research 25* (2) (2001); 232.

Wellman, Barry. *Networks in the Global Village: Life in Contemporary Communities*. Boulder, CO: Westview Press, 1999.

Williams, Thomas. *Who Is My Neighbor: Personalism and the Foundations of Human Rights*. Washington DC: Catholic University of America Press, 2012.

Witherington, Ben. *Conflict and Community in Corinth: a Socio-Rhetorical Commentary on 1 and 2 Corinthians*. Grand Rapids, MI: W.B. Eerdmans, 1995.

Zirschky, Andrew. "The Eucharist and Young Adults Project: An Exploration of the Meaning of Communion Practices in the Faith Lives of Nazarene Young Adults Ages 17 to 26," unpublished manuscript.

CPSIA information can be obtained
at www.ICGtesting.com
Printed in the USA
LVHW04s0704290818
588438LV00004B/4/P